Laurence King Publishing

The Pattern Sourcebook
A century of surface design
Drusilla Cole

Contents

Introduction

The Pattern Sourcebook is a collection of diverse surface pattern designs, which consider colour, texture, image and concept and exemplify what I consider good practice within the context of art and design. The patterns appear on a varied range of products, from wallpaper to fashion fabrics and from ceramics to gift wrap, floor coverings and interior decoration. Nonetheless, the majority of images in the book are of textiles, extant examples either from artist-designers themselves, or from archives or personal collections.

The patterns are arranged by colour rather than by date and so you will often find patterns from the last century juxtaposed with contemporary designs. This clearly demonstrates how patterns from different eras interpret the same inspirations, with widely differing results according to the prevailing style or technical capabilities of the time. The majority of the patterns selected date from the 20th century, when rapid advances in technology and developments in patterning techniques in all arts and crafts were leading the designer forward. A few examples, which caught my eye, date from other eras. Most contemporary designs and artwork are created with powerful computer systems, traditional hand-rendered media or any combination of the two. In this book, however, there is a concentration on hand-generated patterns, however subsequently produced.

Hand screen printing was introduced in the 1930s and took a prominent place in the production of printed textiles. A few pioneering manufacturers, such as Allan Walton, saw the value of screen printing in terms of both creative and commercial considerations. Their innovations paved the way for the artist-designer textiles of the 1940s, especially those initiated by Zika Ascher's textile-printing company. Mechanized screen printing was introduced in the late 1950s and rotary screen printing in the 1960s, which once more revolutionized the industry. Transfer printing was a new technique that appeared in the 1980s and it continues in use, especially for synthetic goods and T-shirts. Today's technology favours digital or computer controlled laser printing, with dyes projected directly onto the cloth.

A remarkable series of designs of particular note are the ones based on the X-ray crystallography of atomic structure. These patterns were first observed during scientific analysis work, and it was the idea of one leading researcher, Dr Helen Magaw, that they could be used without much alteration as inspiration to produce designs for various surfaces. The idea was taken up by the Festival Pattern Group, who used contributions from manufacturers from all over Britain of textiles, carpets, plastics, wallcoverings, ceramics and glass patterned with designs inspired by crystallography, as furnishings for the restaurant and exhibition centres of the hugely influential Festival of Britain, which took place in London in 1951. The legacy of these designs was the plethora of motifs based on molecular and microorganism shapes that popularized textiles throughout the 1950s.

Many of the patterns shown here are taken from pattern books housed in museum archives, such as the Macclesfield Silk Museum and the Worcester Porcelain Museum. Often discarded in the past, these compendiums of designs and pattern samples are now carefully preserved and are a magnificent source of reference. In most cases, however, the artists' or designers' names are absent, which leads to a great number of examples being labelled as 'anonymous' in this book. Nevertheless, their work is worthy of recognition.

Another series of textiles worth mentioning is drawn from an archive of Bilbille & Co. samples dated 1959–60. Bilbille & Co. was a Parisian fabric-sampling house that predicted trends in textiles. These samples were presented to leading French couture fashion houses for consideration and are a unique reference material as they allow an appreciation of the actual colours, texture and fibres used in their creation.

A different group of patterns are *croquis* – the hand-painted designs that are produced to sell a pattern. These mostly date from the late 1960s to the early 1970s and are ideas for designs, ready to be adapted and put into repeat, as and when they are sold.

Also of interest are a number of *katagami*, which are antique Japanese mulberry-paper stencil patterns, traditionally used to print kimono and obi patterns onto lengths of fabric. Cutting the stencils is extremely skilled and dexterous work and the resulting *katagami* are extraordinary and beautiful objects in their own right.

Surface pattern designs generally take their inspiration from nature and the world around us, or are based on geometric or abstract shapes, but occasionally with an emphasis on propaganda, such as the remarkable designs produced by the artists and designers of the Soviet Union in the late 1920s and early 1930s. Their designs focus on utilitarian issues, such as the mobilization of the workforce and the mechanization of agriculture, and have a powerful immediacy and grandeur.

At the very beginning of the 20th century, synthetic dyestuffs were newly discovered and were being successfully introduced into the textile dyeing and printing industries. Previously, dyeing had relied on quantities of plant, mineral or insect-based matter, used in combination with certain metal salts or mordants and a variety of noxious or unsavoury necessary additions. A very high level of skill was needed to produce colours that were fast to washing and light. In the late 1800s, dyestuffs

began to be produced synthetically using chemicals that were relatively consistent in quality and much easier to apply. This development had enormous consequences and led to the profusion of colours that we take for granted today.

At that time, the process of printing textiles ranged from roller printing, which is still used today for large runs of fabric, to the highly skilled method of block printing, which gave excellent results, but was time consuming and was little used commercially after the 1940s. Throughout the text, the means of printing or reproduction has been identified wherever possible. These processes represent the many long hours of preparation before a pattern can be produced, and I want to acknowledge that debt to unseen and unsung craftsmen and craftswomen who translate the designs onto cloth, china, glass or other materials, as well as to the artists and designers who originate the patterns themselves. It is their combined artistry and dedication to the task in hand that has made these patterns so absorbing and beautiful to behold.

My intention in writing this book was to share a selection of some of my favourite patterns gathered from a variety of sources worldwide. There are so many wonderful patterns in existence that I have only been able to include a fraction of them – but I hope you will enjoy them too and find them inspirational.

Opposite
Rita Trefois
2007
Often inspired by ancient Chinese textile decoration, this Belgian batik artist produces wall hangings on cotton and other fibres, using a combination of wax and overdyeing techniques.

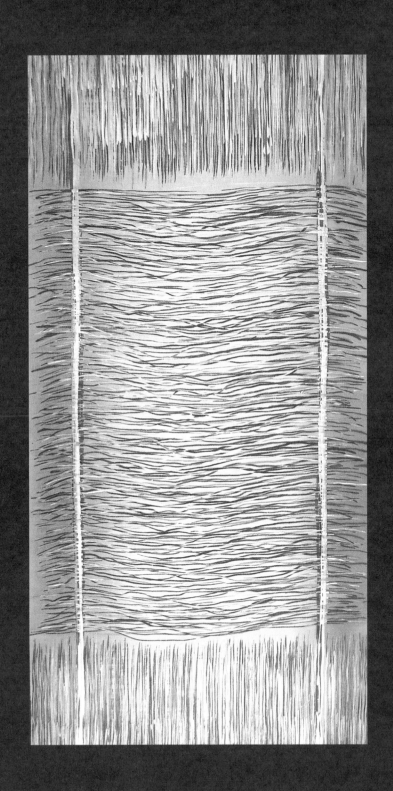

Anonymous (French School)
1940s–50s
Depicting the zodiac, this design is drawn in the style of the gifted littérateur and artist, Jean Cocteau, and originates from France.

Rob Ryan
Stepping Stones, 2007
The result of the artist's painstaking hand-cutting of paper, this intricate and delicate design has been further developed as a limited-edition screen print.

Drusilla Cole
1998
Random geometric shapes in masking fluid and inks
have been used to create a design suitable for fabrics
or gift wrap.

**Anonymous for John Barlow
of Macclesfield**
1904
Woven on a Jacquard loom in deep blue silk, this
is a sample of a design for a muffler or cravat and
features shells, a popular motif of the time.

Anonymous
1940s
A gouache design for a textile featuring a sporting theme, with images of boxers, skiers, fencers and others engaged in their particular leisure activity.

Anonymous
1930s–40s
Understated blue roses in a restrained pattern cover
this roller-printed French linen fabric, designed for
curtains and upholstery.

Robin Stewart
Cotton Tuft, 1977
A hand screen-printed wallpaper by Robin Stewart
Handprints Ltd, featuring a pattern derived from
a microscopic view of cotton fibres. The repeat
has to be exact both horizontally and vertically for
wallpaper and this complex pattern must certainly
have been a lot of fun to do!

Susan Bosence
1980s
Pleated and tightly sewn, this is a section of *shibori*
tied cotton fabric after it has been dyed in indigo.
Even though it is meant to be undone to expose the
white undyed areas, the cloth has a most pleasing
aspect just as it is.

Mark Hearld
Doveflight, 2007
Based on the artist's celebrated lithographic
and linocut prints, this design is enhanced by the
way that the intertwining colours and images
suggest movement.

Ella Doran
Scrunched Ice, 2007
A piece of blue paper has been crumpled and photographed before being digitally manipulated into a clever *trompe l'oeil* gift wrap. *Trompe l'oeil* images purposefully create the optical illusion that two-dimensional items appear to be three-dimensional.

Phyllis Barron and Dorothy Larcher
1920s–30s
This skilful design on linen by these two craftswomen has been dyed with indigo, and then discharged with nitric acid using a hand-printing block. The rediscovered techniques are the result of their intensive historical research into 19th-century dyeing and printing manuals, located in the libraries of the Victoria and Albert Museum, London.

Linda Brassington
1980s
A length of cotton voile fabric that has a complex pattern produced entirely by hand. It was first block printed with iron rust to give the black 'keyline', or boundary line, then wax resist was added to maintain the white areas before it was finally overdyed in indigo to give the blue background.

Anonymous
1980s
Wax-printed cloth is based on the appearance of traditional Indonesian batik cloth but employs a quicker and cheaper method. It uses a resin paste printed onto both sides of the cotton cloth, which is then dyed in indigo. The cloth is afterwards treated mechanically to produce the cracking effect, characteristic of a real batik or wax print.

Kate Faulkner
Carnation, 1875
Designed by Kate Faulkner, *Carnation* was the first machine-printed wallpaper design that Morris & Co. ever produced. William Morris had wanted to use the machine process to produce at least a percentage of his wallpaper output, but only one other design was ever machine-produced during the lifetime of Morris, which was *Merton*, also designed by Kate Faulkner.

Phyllis Barron
1920s
This textile sample was indigo-dyed and discharged
using nitric acid, a hazardous procedure requiring
considerable skill. Dyeing with indigo is rarely
a straightforward affair, as there are so many
variables involved. Nonetheless, this pioneering
craftswoman mastered the art and produced many
exceptional designs and patterns printed and dyed
with the distinctive blue colour of indigo dyestuff.

(Probably) Marthilde Flögl
c.1925
Marthilde Flögl was a pupil of Josef Hoffmann and
worked in the Wiener Werkstätte textile design
department, producing over 120 patterns for
apparel and furnishings. Her designs probably
included this carefully composed pattern, which
was printed onto silk and intended for dress fabric.

Phyllis Barron and Dorothy Larcher
1932
Heavy natural linen, hand-printed with indigo using a wooden block designed and cut by Phyllis Barron. It was created for curtains for the Fellows Common Room of Girton College, Cambridge.

Joseph–Theodore Deck
c.1865
One of the leading French ceramicists of his day,
Deck was attracted to the design and techniques of
Islamic wares, and designed ceramics influenced by
this style, some of which he presented at the 1862
London Exhibition.

Anonymous for Bilbille & Co., Paris
1959–60
Overlapping blue and white china plates have been printed onto cotton poplin in this pleasing fabric sample directed towards Parisian couturiers.

Drusilla Cole
2008
A digital design derived from an antique *katagami*,
or Japanese paper stencil. The pattern used is
intended to illustrate rain and pools of water.

Anonymous for Langley Printworks
1922–25
Termed a 'rayonee' pattern, this fabric sample was
produced by a process similar to that used to create
marbled designs on paper and fabric. Apparently,
the process involved using 'an intensely foul
smelling animal product'!

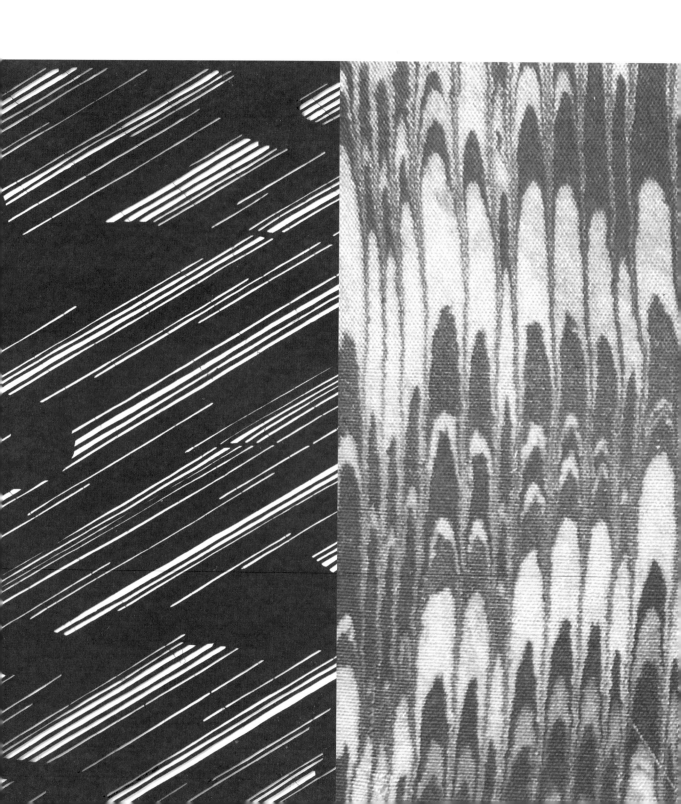

Henry Moore for Ascher Textiles
Treble Clef, Zigzag and Oval Safety Pins,
1946–47
Ascher Textiles produced luxury fabrics for the
fashion industry and, during the 1940s, they
commissioned designs from leading international
artists – in this case, the eminent sculptor Henry
Moore. The motifs used in the design are developed
from his numerous sketches, and include a garden
rake and an insect hovering above a stylized pond.

Anonymous
1960s
A length of heat transfer-printed polyester fabric,
featuring rather peculiarly coloured flowers that
have been designed using the recently introduced
photomontage technique.

Anonymous
1930s–40s
Floral motifs decorate a quarter design for a ladies handkerchief for the home market, hand block-printed onto rayon. Initially known as 'artificial silk', rayon (or viscose, as it known today) is made from regenerated cellulose fibres, harvested from tree pulp and cotton waste, and at the time was approximately half the price of silk.

Anonymous
1970s
Hand screen-printed in France, this blue floral-sprigged fabric is an example of a 'Provencal' fabric. Contemporary artisans still reference the original antique textile documents to find new designs and patterns for fabrics and textile accessories.

Anonymous
1950s
Vignettes of donkeys, local people in ethnic dress
and simple flowers decorate a bright and cheerful
cotton dress fabric. A design such as this might have
served to remind travellers of their holidays abroad.

Clarice Cliff
Rudyard, 1933
One of the *Fantastique* landscape patterns by this well-known and highly collectible ceramicist. The pattern is that of a stylized tree with a dappled green trunk and pink and blue pendulous foliage.

Edward Bawden
Night and Day, 1957
A screen-printed cotton panel designed by one
of Britain's most influential artists of the mid 20th
century, who produced a wide variety of artwork,
ranging from advertising material for Shell, to his
work as an official war artist.

Phyllis Barron and Dorothy Larcher
Carnac, 1920s–30s
Inspired by the stone carvings found in Carnac, France, this is an appealing design of discharged indigo. Archivist Robin Tanner wrote: 'The stuffs upon which the designs were printed and the dyes used were so completely and sensitively understood that there was an inevitability about the work… there was always perfect harmony between the fibre, the dye and the block.'

Phyllis Barron and Dorothy Larcher
Hazlitt, 1920s–30s
An attractive hand block-printed cotton fabric by
these enterprising craftswomen, who rediscovered
the complex technique of discharging indigo dye via
nitric acid. When printed on unbleached linen *Hazlitt*
made suitable prints for upholstery and curtains.

Alexander Girard for máXimo inc.
Eden, 1964
One of the most important names in mid 20th-
century textiles, American designer Alexander
Girard used traditional folk art to infuse colour,
whimsy and humour into vibrant modern design.

Anonymous
c.1880
A fabulous hand-painted watercolour design for
a large ewer in a rich Middle Eastern style, which
would be hand-decorated to imitate cloisonné
enamels. This type of shape and decoration would
have been considered very exotic and mysterious
at the time.

Anonymous
c.1880
Lithographically printed in two colours, this blue ceramic tile would have been one of several similar tiles decorating the surround of an ornate fireplace.

Anonymous
c.1910
A Jacquard design woven in vibrant blue, gold and black silks, featuring a feather-like structure around a floating orb. This sample was probably intended to be used for a gentleman's fancy waistcoat or cravat.

Marie-Noëlle Fontan
Chichicaste, 2007
Marie-Noëlle Fontan is a native of Toulouse, France. She lived for over a decade in Guatemala and now lives and works in Paris, France. Her unique way of working is to collect seedpods, leaves, roots and barks, assemble and dry them, then weave them into delicate and evocative structures, pierced by sudden brightly coloured threads.

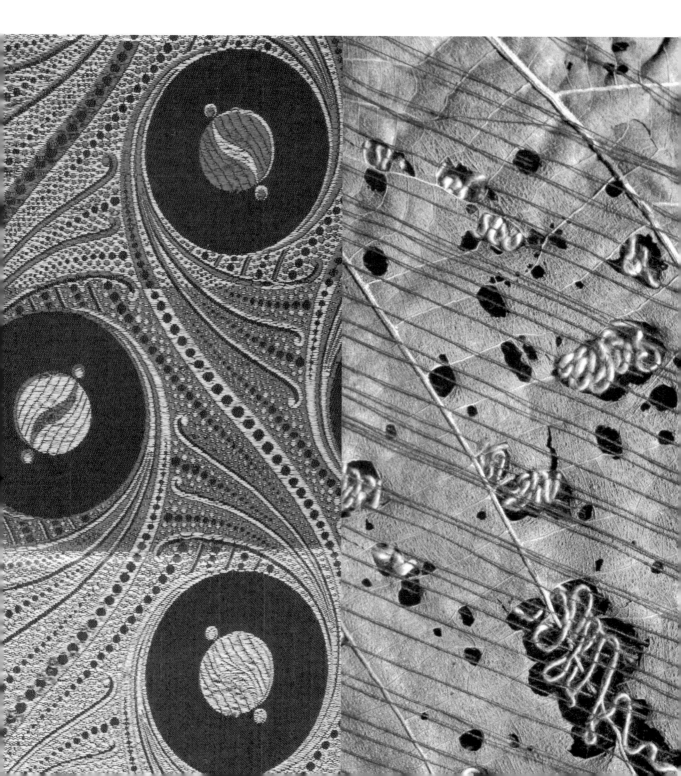

Hannah Firmin
Winter, 2006
An evocative design for greeting cards, which
was developed via a complex lino print and
collage technique.

**Kathie Winkle for James Broadhurst
& Sons Ltd**

Concord, 1960s

Kathie Winkle was a talented painter who became
responsible for all Broadhurst's pattern designs
from the late 1950s until the mid 1970s. Her crisp
geometric patterns were a clear departure from
the more usual floral motifs found on ceramics of
the time.

Frank Ormrod
Belvoir, 1935–37
A roller-printed linen furnishing fabric, which references the elements and colouring of a much older textile document, in particular, the shades of indigo blue and soga brown and the geometric patterning in the background.

Anonymous
1930s
This swatch of Jacquard woven roses contains two different colour-ways, showing it was woven as a sample rather than a finished piece.

Anonymous for Langley Printworks
1935–39
Paratroopers descend out of a clear blue sky in this
hand-printed wood-block design for a handkerchief.

Anonymous for Langley Printworks
1935–39
Featuring dancing ladies in wide striped skirts, this hand block-printed design in three colours is for a handkerchief.

Anonymous
1950s
Overlapping brushstrokes of colour feature in this
striking screen-printed cotton shirting fabric, which
was manufactured in the USA.

James Pegg
2008
Inspired by the glass and optic artist Justin Knowles, this hand screen-printed fabric sample is brilliantly coloured in acid blues and turquoises.

William De Morgan

c.1870

A vibrant tile design by this important ceramicist.
In the late 1870s, De Morgan built a kiln in the
basement of his home in Fitzroy Square, London,
to work on his experimental lustres and glazes.
Unfortunately, his enthusiasm led to a fire that
destroyed the roof, about which 'the landlord did
not seem at all amiable'.

Anonymous for Bilbille & Co., Paris
1959–60
Flock-printed roses screen-printed onto navy
moss-textured viscose feature in this fabric
sample from Paris.

William Burges
1890
Rebuilt as a country retreat for the third Marquis of
Bute, this is a detail of a painted ceiling from Castle
Coch, South Wales. Here, William Burges created
lavish and opulent themed interiors; rich with
hand-painted murals and fantastic neo-medieval
style detailing.

William Morris
Strawberry Thief, 1870s
Mainly dyed in indigo with red and green highlights, this delicately coloured fabric sample from the master artisan William Morris has been discharge-printed by hand. The pattern was inspired by the need to keep the thrushes off the strawberries at Morris's country house, Kelmscott.

Francesca Chiorando
2008
Created using segments of the artist's own printed
and pleated fabric, this section was repeated and
printed digitally to produce a structured pattern.

Francesca Chiorando
2008
Digitally manipulated into repeat, using mirror
images of sections of her own printed fabric,
this dynamic and intriguing pattern is strangely
reminiscent of a psychiatrist's ink-blot.

Francesca Chiorando
Beach–Break, 2008
Waves of blue and bronze enliven this printed and
painted fabric sample. The artist comments: 'Taking
inspiration from the varied scenery of the British
coastline and from found objects washed onto the
shore, I created a vibrant and varied colour palette.
I worked upon the printed fabric manually, pleating
and smocking it.'

J. Sarlandie
c.1925
Made in Limoges, France, by this important
designer-maker, this attractive example of an
enamel vase is in typical early Art Deco style.

Anonymous for Barracks Printing Co.
1960s
Featuring a minimalist geometric design, reflecting the op-art fashions of the period, this is a hand-painted gouache *croquis*, or paper design for a textile.

Emile Gallé
c.1899
In the spring of 1898, the celebrated French
artist Emile Gallé patented the technique of glass
marquetry. The process involved the incorporation
of glass fragments of various thickness, shapes
and colours into the still malleable glass mass. This
bottle is decorated with an orchid design executed
in glass marquetry.

Anonymous
1954
Made of rayon brocade and woven on a Jacquard loom, this sample features a very elegantly portrayed bouquet of flowers on a small spotted background.

Anonymous for Bilbille & Co., Paris
1959–60
Blue pure silk chiffon has been screen-printed with an animated painterly style design as a sample for a French fashion house.

S. M. Slade for British Celanese Ltd
1951
Printed onto fine filament, acetate rayon crêpe, this design is based on the crystal structure diagram of afwillite. It was at the suggestion of Dr Helen Magaw, from Birkbeck College, London, that crystallography, the determining of the arrangement of atoms, should be used to inspire pattern designs for the very important Festival of Britain exhibition.

Marie Chart
1952
A screen-printed sample of fabric manufactured by Heal & Son, London, featuring a rather outdated pattern of oval vignettes, which contain flowers and leaves. A smaller-scale pattern of white dots and isolated leaves surrounds each panel on a duck-egg blue background.

Seiko Kinoshita
Blue Bird, 2007
A site-specific installation consisting of 580 bird-shaped pieces of hand-dyed, woven paper yarn. The work is intended to bring harmony and a sense of movement between the floors of the Sheffield Central Library building. The artist comments: 'I was inspired by the book *The Blue Bird* by Maeterlinck and imagined the birds to be flying up the staircase towards the beautiful skylight window above.'

Anonymous for Horrockses Fabrics
1950s
Painterly spots of turquoise appear all over this
screen-printed dress fabric made by Horrockses,
who were one of Britain's largest cotton
manufacturers. The company produced a huge
range of cotton fabrics from 1791 until the 1960s,
winning international awards for their products.

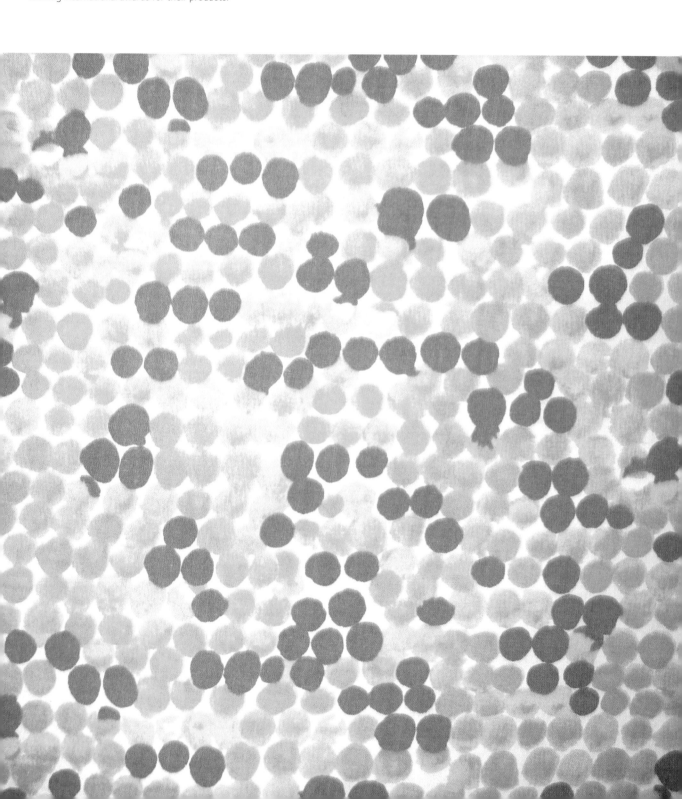

Linda Sjunnesson for Spira
Eden, 2006
Bold blue passion flowers, leaves and tendrils combine in a crisp and stylish Scandinavian screen print for furnishing fabrics.

Phyllis Barron and Dorothy Larcher
Diagonal, 1920s–30s
Labelled 'much faded with long use', this is an indigo
discharge print on undyed, hand-spun and hand-
woven Indian cotton. Many of these craftswomen's
hand-cut wooden printing blocks were in use for
many years, printing all manner of cloths, which
they sold or used in their own home.

Dagobert Peche
Tausendblumen, 1922
In 1915, Dagobert Peche joined the Wiener Werkstätte, the artist's co-operative, and became one of its most creative members, designing several thousand objects before his early death in 1923. His astonishing output included ceramics, furnishings, frames and mirrors, jewellery, wallpaper and textiles, all exuding the lightness of touch and attention to detail that characterized his work.

Anonymous for Langley Printworks
1900–12
Roses and sprigs of leaves in a design intended for dresses and blouses have been hand block-printed in a proof taken on paper (called a printer's 'fent') to test the registration of wood-blocks for the design.

Chloe Geary
2006
Focusing on her drawings of details of windows
in New York buildings, this artist has produced a
digitally printed pattern, where striped lines create
the sense of the tall buildings.

Chloe Geary
Paris, 2008
Silk scarves, digitally printed with images derived from a range of illustrations titled *Paint the Town*. The artist comments: 'I think Paris has a higgledy-piggledy, shabby romance and I wanted to idealize the mood you remember when you visit it and capture it using colour and line. All of my work is hand-drawn and then combined with blocks of flat digital colour and manipulated to create a pattern.'

Rachel Goodchild
Swallows, 2008
Black art paper has been hand-cut with scissors
and enhanced with silver pencil to produce an
evocative design for cards and gift wrap. The artist
comments: 'I saw this flight of swallows against
the amazing blue sky and I just had to see if I could
create something similar in a design.'

Pippa Caley
2006
This dazzling pattern has been embroidered by means of an Irish machine, which produces many pleasing varieties of flat embroidery work. The needle can vibrate towards the right or the left, or be made to zigzag across a central line by controlling the hand or knee levers.

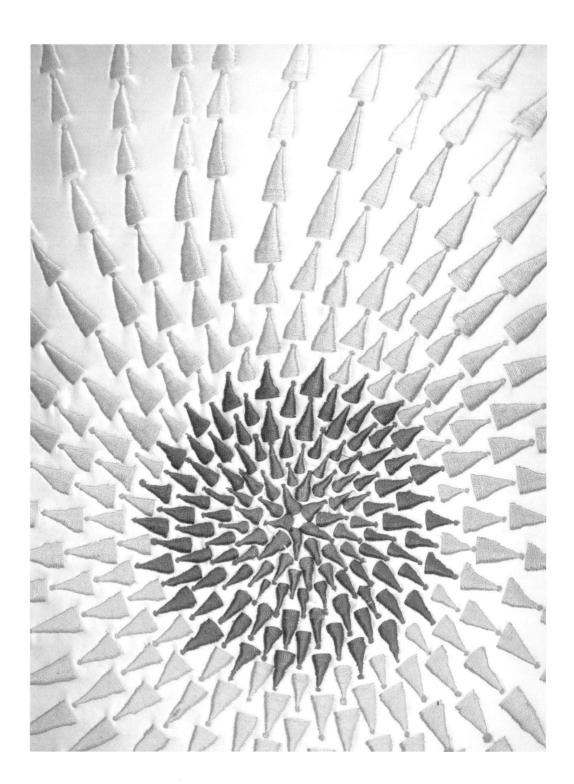

Ella Doran
Disco Blue, 1990s
Bright spots of light gleam in the dark on a
digitally produced gift wrap, which is based on
this designer's innovative use of photographs.

Florence Broadhurst
1963–77
Oversized naturalistic flower motifs combine with
irregular spots in a monochrome hand screen-
printed wallcovering.

George Aitchison II
*Detail of The Narcissus Hall, Leighton House,
London*, 1877–81
Architect George Aitchison II, designer of Leighton
House, created interiors for grand London houses
owned by wealthy art patrons. He devised these
door architraves with incised gilded decoration,
which are repeated throughout the house. The
vibrant blue tiles are the work of celebrated Arts
and Crafts ceramicist, William De Morgan.

Florence Broadhurst
1960s–70s
A furnishing fabric hand screen-printed with a stylized repeating fan motif by this prolific designer who, at the time, monopolized the quality end of the Australian hand screen-printed wallcovering market, and exported worldwide.

Kim Barnett
2006
Wild and crazy images combined with expert digital techniques characterize this contemporary avant-garde designer's patterns. In this example, sea creatures are frolicking on a digital print for home furnishings.

Reiko Sudo for Nuno Corporation
Walnuts, 2008
This delicate and detailed working drawing by an innovative Japanese firm uses the walnut tree as inspiration. The designer comments: 'In some countries, people tell fortunes with walnuts or use them as charms for safe childbirth or even toss them at wedding celebrations. Thus walnut leaves make a perfect auspicious motif for a ballroom, to be realized as a dense-piled Wilton rug.'

Anonymous for Bilbille & Co., Paris
1959–60
Floral designs have always been popular motifs
and in the late 1950s and 60s many varied and
discordant colour schemes were tried out, perhaps
not always harmoniously, as is the case with this
woollen serge sample.

Hannah Firmin
Spring, 2006
Nesting birds, tulips, snake's head fritillaries, even a spider and a snail are pieced together in this design for greeting cards. The pattern is derived from several original linocuts, which are hand-printed onto coloured tissue paper before being cut up and reassembled.

Anonymous for Bilbille & Co., Paris
1959–60
A multicoloured all-over print nearly obliterates
the teardrop *boteh* motif at the heart of this
satin-weave cotton sample.

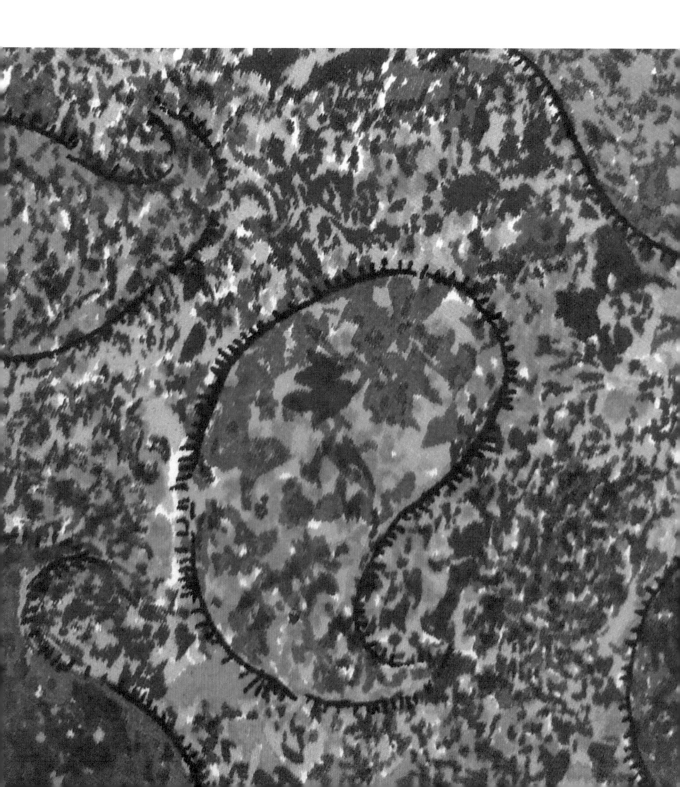

**Enoch Boulton for Royal Crown Derby
Porcelain Co.**
Mattajade, 1932
Featuring hand-applied jade green 'waved' ground
and enamelled decoration enhanced by a gold
overprint, this is a fine example of a porcelain bowl.
Its designer, Enoch Boulton, is only now beginning
to be recognized as a significant force in innovative
ceramic design.

Pippa Caley
2007
This artist's embellished bespoke products offer a
splash of colour and texture to any interior space.
Her creations range from chairs and bed quilts to
textile wallcoverings.

**Ian Fraser for Tootal Broadhurst
Lee Co. Ltd**
Locomotion, 1956
Depictions of ancient and contemporary trains,
planes and transport of all sorts were a favourite
theme during this period.

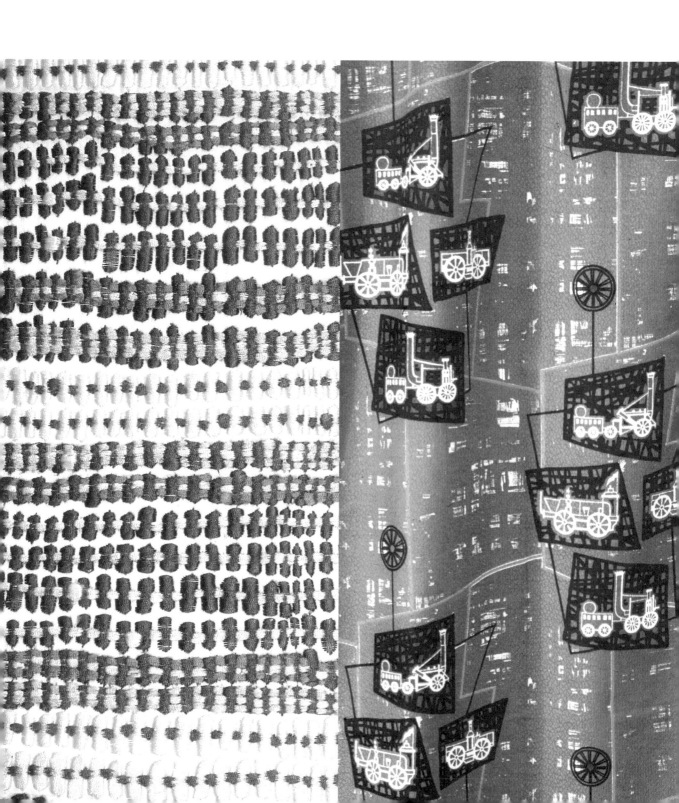

Anonymous
1930s
A German design in gouache on paper, featuring tiny tortoises on a black, subtly patterned background. The tortoise motif is a favourite symbol in many countries and often represents themes such as long or eternal life and revered old age.

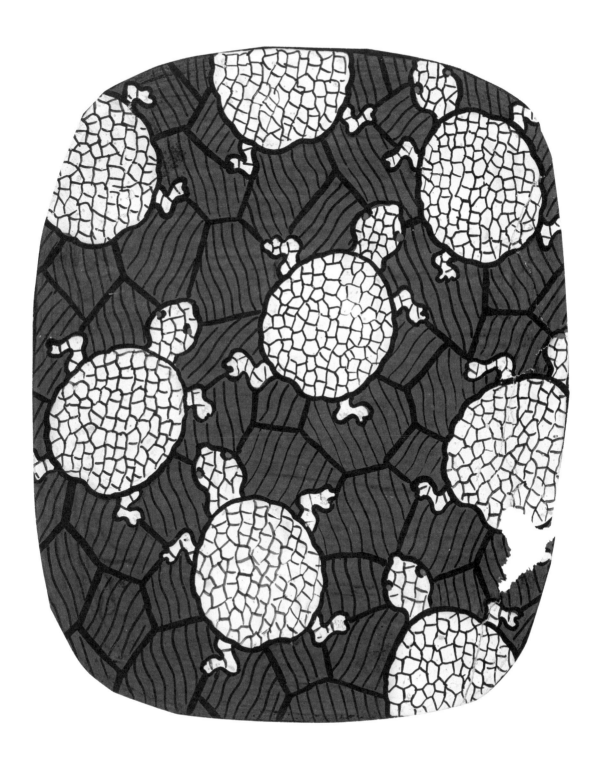

Chloe Geary
2007
Derived from a range of her own illustrations
entitled *Paint the Town*, this artist's patterns use
her sketches, digitally manipulated into repeat. The
artist comments: 'I thought New York City was full
of sleek angles and polished windows and I wanted
to idealize this mood and capture it in the work
using colour and line.'

Anonymous
1950s
A screen-printed cotton furnishing fabric executed in the 'Festival of Britain style', which came into fashion after a successful post-war exhibition held on the South Bank, London, in 1951.

Anonymous for Royal Worcester Porcelain
1922
A page from a tableware pattern book illustrating
hand-decorated teacups and saucers. The shape of
the flowers is typical of the designs on textiles and
ceramics of the time, and follows the naïve style of
decoration made popular by Parisian designer Paul
Poiret's workshop, the Atelier Martine.

Pat Albeck for Cavendish Textiles Ltd
Patricia, 1974
Simple yet bold pink and white flowers are scattered over this screen-printed linen to make a very effective design for furnishing fabrics.

Josef Frank
Poisons, 1940s
Perhaps this master pattern-maker's most
significant skill was his use of colours – contrasting
and complementary, they dazzle and excite the
eye. Combined with his beautifully observed
botanical illustrations, he produced designs that
have remained popular for over 60 years.

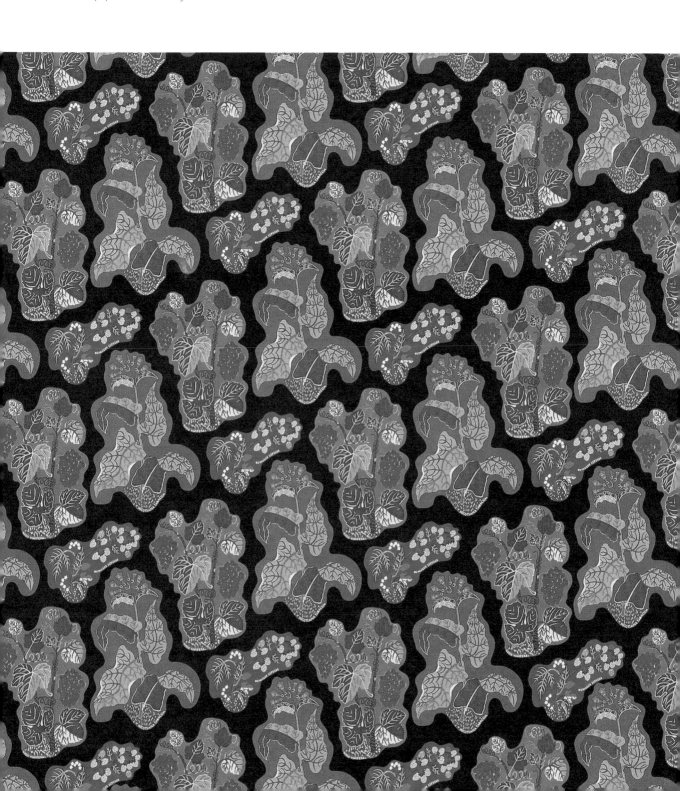

Florence Broadhurst
1960s–70s
This enterprising Australian artist and entrepreneur has depicted intertwining galloping horses in an ingenious repeating design for wallpaper.

Afro Basaldella
1957
An abstract pattern for a machine screen-printed furnishing fabric produced by David Whitehead Fabrics Ltd of Lancashire, England. The firm's philosophy was stated as being to cater for 'those vast sections of humanity in which the emphasis is on cheapness and serviceability'.

Marianne Straub
1960
Woven from wool and cotton, this fabric is by Swiss-born designer Marianne Straub, an innovative textile designer of the mid 20th century. Her biographer, Mary Schoeser, wrote: 'Marianne Straub is one of the few designers of mass-produced textiles who has embraced both design tasks successfully. In doing so she has shaped public taste and set standards for industrial production.'

Anonymous for Bilbille & Co., Paris
1959–60
Very characteristic of its time, this floral design
features boldly hand-drawn images of roses and
leaves in black, screen-printed with a rather garish
palette of yellow, orange and green.

Marianne Straub for Warner & Sons
Surrey, 1951
Based on the crystal structure of afwillite, this is a
Jacquard woven wool and cotton furnishing fabric.
Crystallography allowed scientists to work out the
arrangement of atoms within molecules, and it is
these structures that designers used as inspiration
to create woven and printed patterns.

Alec Hunter for Warner & Sons
Harwell, 1951
Featuring a pattern based on the crystal structure diagram of china clay this is a Jacquard woven furnishing fabric. At the time, *The Times* declared: 'It is a pleasant change to dissociate the atom from the idea of a destructive bomb and to apply it to the creation of things of beauty.'

Herbert Woodman for Warner & Sons
Harwood, 1938
A screen-printed figured linen fabric of shell-like leaves and sprays, by an in-house designer who worked in Britain during the 1930s.

Eileen Bell
1957
A machine screen-printed furnishing fabric
manufactured by David Whitehead Fabrics Ltd,
featuring a semi-naturalistic design of fruit and
musical instruments arranged around a pillar. The
designer, Eileen Bell, was a prolific artist who was
still applying paint to canvas in her mid-nineties.

Anonymous for Turnbull & Stockdale Ltd
1954
Two printed furnishing fabrics in typical post-war patterns – one using stylized vintage locomotion images and the other a woven Jacquard fabric in jagged stripes and muted colours.

Angie Lewin
Seedheads, 2007
Based on the seed-heads which so fascinate this
artist, well known for her exceptional lino and
lithographic prints, this is a highly regulated pattern
for wallpapers.

Maija Fagerlund
Secret Garden, 2007
Drawing some of her inspiration from old wallpapers and gardens, this Finnish designer comments: 'I have first drawn the sketches with ink and pen, and made the repeat and colouring with a computer.'

Anonymous
1870s
This beautiful pattern is a hand block-printed cotton *palempore*, or bedcover from Futtygurh, Bengal. It was one of many fabrics compiled into several volumes entitled *Textile Manufactures and Costumes of the People of India* by Dr J. Forbes Watson in the 1870s. This was probably the first authentic and systematic record of the textile industry in 19th-century India.

Anonymous
1870s
In the 1870s, Dr J. Forbes Watson collected many superb samples of naturally dyed and hand block-printed fabrics extant in the subcontinent at the time, into a monumental series of volumes, which were distributed to manufacturers in Britain with the intention of inspiring designers and pattern-makers.

Edward Bawden
Woodpigeon, 1927
A lithographically printed wallpaper that features vignettes of church spires and wood pigeons seen through windows of leaves. Bawden's designs were often based on his own expert linocuts.

John Piper for Arthur Sanderson and Sons
Stones of Bath, 1960
Designed as part of an initiative to use some of
Britain's best-loved artists to produce designs for
screen-printed furnishing fabrics and wallpapers,
this example is typical of John Piper's layered,
multicoloured style of working. It incorporates
elements from buildings seen in and around the
city of Bath, England.

Susan Bosence
1950s–60s
Somewhat resembling fishes, an abstract design by this gifted artist and craftswoman has been hand block-printed, paste-resist patterned and overdyed in manganese brown, a mineral-based dye.

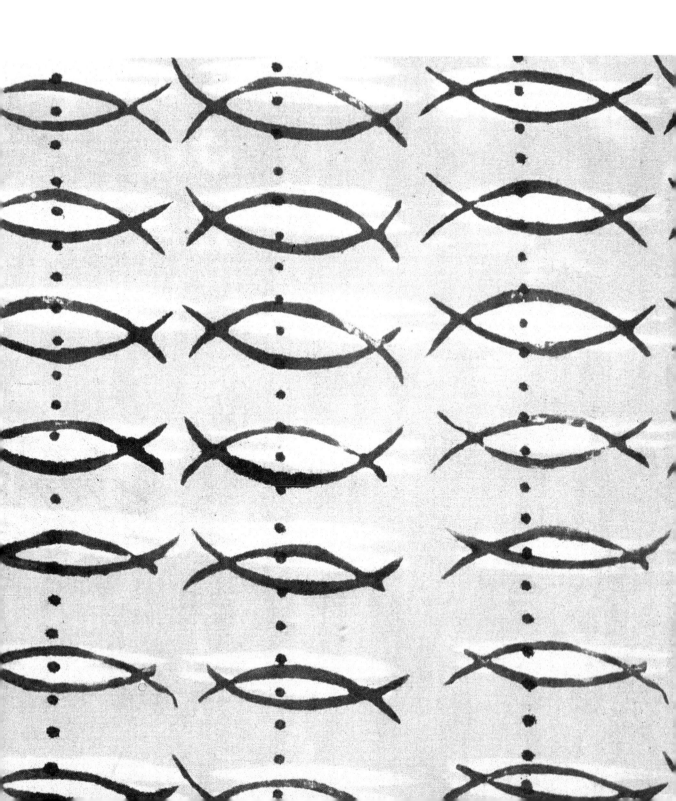

Anonymous for Langley Printworks
1951–52
A quarter design for a screen-printed silk headscarf,
featuring carefully drawn lilies, and the words
'Bermuda Easter Lilies' written along the edge. Lilies
are among the favourite motifs of flower painters.

Anonymous for Wade, Heath & Co.
c.1928
Painted in an imitation Egyptian style, this hand-painted glazed earthenware jug has asymmetrical panels on each side. Egyptian style designs became very popular after the discovery and opening of Tutankhamen's tomb in 1922.

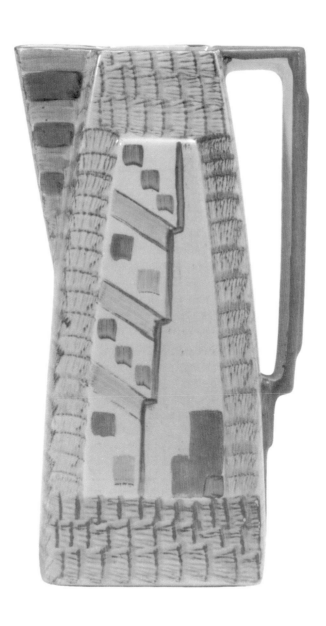

Sir Hugh Casson for Midwinter Pottery
Cannes, 1954
Based on sketches by Sir Hugh Casson of French
street scenes, this design is part of the *Riviera*
series, which quickly became one of the most
popular print and enamel designs. Resident
Midwinter designer Jessie Tait worked on translating
the sketches to fit the shapes of the ceramics.

Anonymous
1960s
Gardens, exotic or otherwise, have always been a popular subject for textiles, and this vibrant screen-printed silk is an interesting example of the genre.

35

Fagerlund
, 2006

Sharply delineated leaves and berries are scattered across this textile design. The artist comments: 'Puuska means a kind of wind in Finnish and a windy autumn day and falling leaves had inspired me to make this pattern. I have first drawn the motifs by hand and then made the repeat and colouring with computer.'

Anonymous (French School)
1950s
Currently very out of favour, smoking-related images were previously occasionally used as design motifs, as pictured in this hand-painted gouache textile design.

Maija Fagerlund
Helle, 2007
Working in her hometown of Helsinki, this Finnish
designer has produced a range of patterns for
furnishing and fashion fabrics, as well as applications
that are more unusual, such as designs for
wheelchair fabrics.

Aino-Maija Metsola for Marimekko
Juhannustaika, 2007
Originally designed in wet-on-wet watercolours,
this screen-printed furnishing fabric has retained
its painterly quality.

Inga Karlsson for Spira
Puls, 2008
Alternating and interlocking shapes in lime green
and white form a crisp and contemporary pattern
for a furnishing fabric – here made up into a
cushion, one of a number of home products
devised by this enterprising Swedish design firm.

Anonymous
1870s
This spectacular fabric is a detail of a hand block-printed cotton fabric, which was part of one of the volumes of samples Dr J. Forbes Watson brought back from India to give British designers and pattern-makers inspiration. The quality of the design, registration and colouration of the hand block printing is outstanding.

Josef Frank
Brazil, 1940s
Brilliantly coloured depictions of exotic fruit and
flowers characterize this multi-talented artist's
textile designs. A keen botany enthusiast, Frank
used nature's own forms and his occasionally gaudy
reinterpretations of their colours to great effect.

Maija Louekari for Marimekko
Dadel, 2007
Using a combination of prominent graphic patterns
and large planes of colour, this Finnish designer
creates an impression of buildings and cityscapes
in her design for a large-scale furnishing fabric.

Charles F. A. Voysey
Fool's Parsley, 1907
A delightful design by this outstanding pattern designer. C. F. A. Voysey was very influential and extremely prolific, designing textiles, wallpapers, furniture, lighting and other decorative items. His architectural works are considered formative in the evolution of the Modern movement. His stated design ideals were 'simplicity, sincerity, repose, directness and frankness'.

Minä Perhonen
Puu, 2005
An embroidered flock of migrating birds in white wool flying over a sunshine yellow background is the unusual fashion fabric created by this enterprising Japanese company. The aim was to portray different individuals merging as a single entity.

Anonymous for Royal Worcester Porcelain
c.1912
A bone china tea plate illustrating how very vibrant
colours were used in the early 20th century.
Repetitive and geometric patterns were printed
onto the china in outline and filled in by hand.

Anonymous for Artesania Talaverana
1960s
Showing Moorish influence, this is a ceramic tile
design in vibrant yellows and blues produced in a
decorative pottery factory at Talavera de la Reina,
Toledo, Spain.

Anonymous
1950s
Brown and orange roses were a popular motif at this time. This version was possibly emulating the celebrated artist Graham Sutherland's well-known *Rose* design.

Anonymous
1950s
Presenting popular images of Royal palaces in
London, Windsor and Edinburgh, this is a quarter
design for a hand screen-printed silk headscarf and
was doubtless intended for the tourist market.

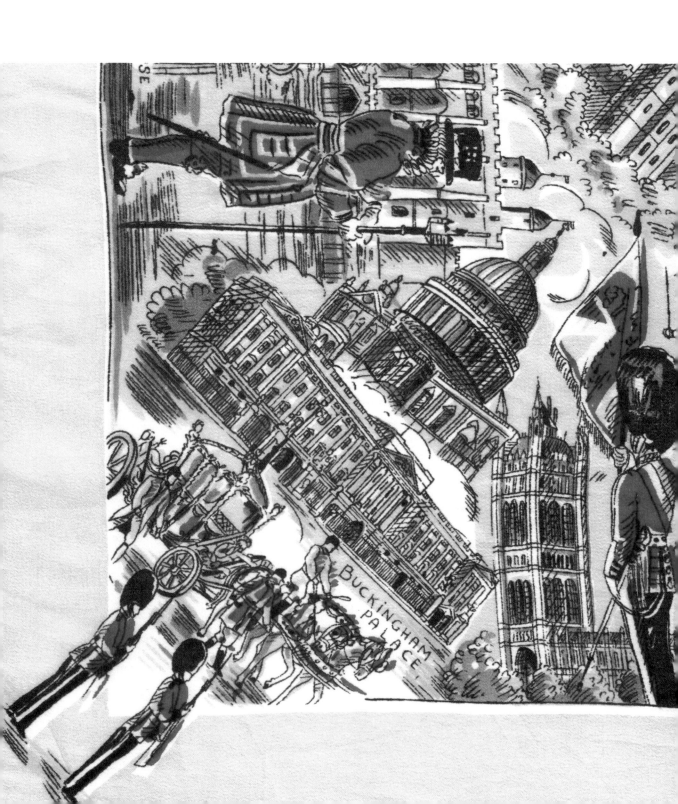

Anonymous for Barracks Printing Co.
1960s
Simple daisy shapes – the decade's quintessential motif – are combined with a 1960s fashionable palette of brown and yellow in this hand-painted gouache design intended for Berne Silks.

Angie Lewin
Dandelion, 2007
Dandelion seed-heads have been stylized and
used as a design motif by this artist, whose
limited-edition linocut and wood engraving prints
are inspired by skeletal plant forms.

Ella Doran
2008
Real daffodils have been artfully arranged,
photographed and digitally manipulated to create
a pleasing pattern for gift wrap.

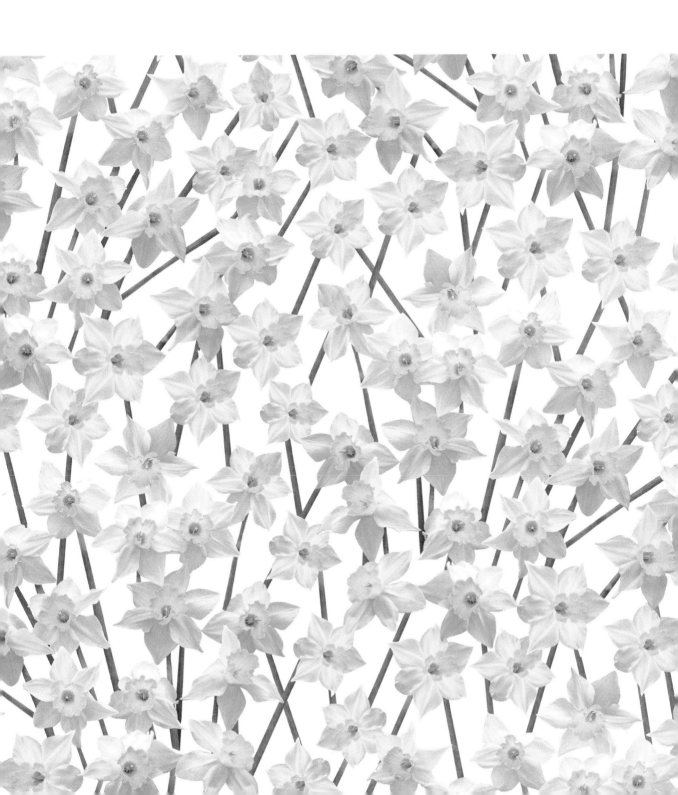

Erja Hirvi for Marimekko
Palma, 2007
Digitally manipulated flowers are used to create
an all-over pattern in this Finnish designer's
brightly coloured furnishing fabric. The bright blue
background shows off the flowers to particularly
good effect.

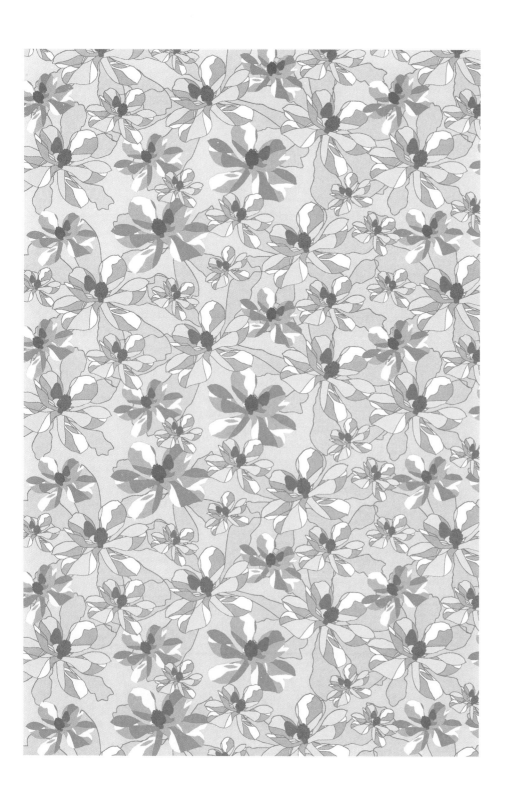

Anonymous for Royal Worcester Porcelain
1885
This richly gilded and jewelled pattern for a plate
was recorded in the Royal Worcester pattern book.
After the porcelain plate was made, the design
would have been hand-painted by a skilled artisan
before being finally fired and burnished.

Edward Raby
c.1895
A delicate and detailed flower border, which is
a hand-painted watercolour design for border
decoration by Edward Raby, who became one of
the most highly paid and well-respected artisans
of his day. This type of colouring was very
fashionable at the turn of the 19th century.

Antoni Gaudí
1900–14
A few of the tiles used in the decoration for Park Güell, Barcelona, which was created by the celebrated Spanish architect Gaudí, famous for his unique and highly individualistic designs.

Richard Riemerschmid
1905
Undulating across a furnishing fabric this pattern is
by the renowned German artist, who was an interior
decorator, furniture designer and architect, and a
leading exponent of *Jugendstil*, or Art Nouveau.

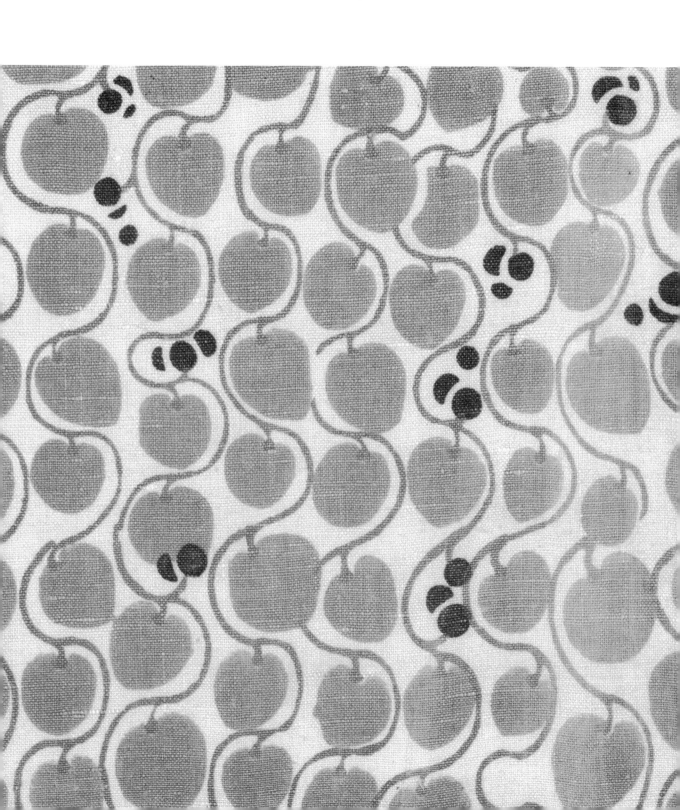

Phyllis Barron and Dorothy Larcher
Dandelion, 1920s–30s
Hand block-printed using an angular black pattern on top of a yellow ground, the black dye was obtained from iron liquor. In its initial policy statement, the Crafts Study Centre that curated their work described the craftswomen as: 'Pioneers who found themselves obliged to rediscover, largely by trial and error, many of the techniques which industrial development had obscured or retarded.'

Anonymous
c.1925
A cotton handkerchief decorated in the Egyptian style, which became popular after the opening of the tomb of Tutankhamen in 1922, by the archaeologist, Dr Howard Carter. The widespread fascination with Egyptian culture meant that various images and artefacts from King Tutankhamen's tomb were used as motifs on textiles, ceramics, jewellery and other objets d'art.

Rachel Goodchild
Leaping Deer, 2006
Referencing Art Deco designs, this pattern is
a collage of scissor-cut shapes prepared from
handmade mulberry paper. Stylized leaping deer
or gazelles became a hallmark of the Art Deco
style of the 1920s and 30s.

Anonymous for Johnson Bros. (Hanley) Ltd
1950s
A detail of a design for tableware, which features a
pleasing illustration of a willow tree with its leaves
being blown around it.

Edward Bawden for The Curwen Press
Sahara, 1928
Appealing and evocative, this lithographic design for
wallpaper by the celebrated and prolific artist and
illustrator Edward Bawden, was developed from one
of his linocuts.

Anonymous for John Barlow of Macclesfield
1904
Macclesfield has had a long association with silk
weaving, dating back over 400 years. In the 1860s,
emigration was encouraged with free travel and
the American silk industry was founded in Paterson,
New Jersey by John Ryle, a Macclesfield man.

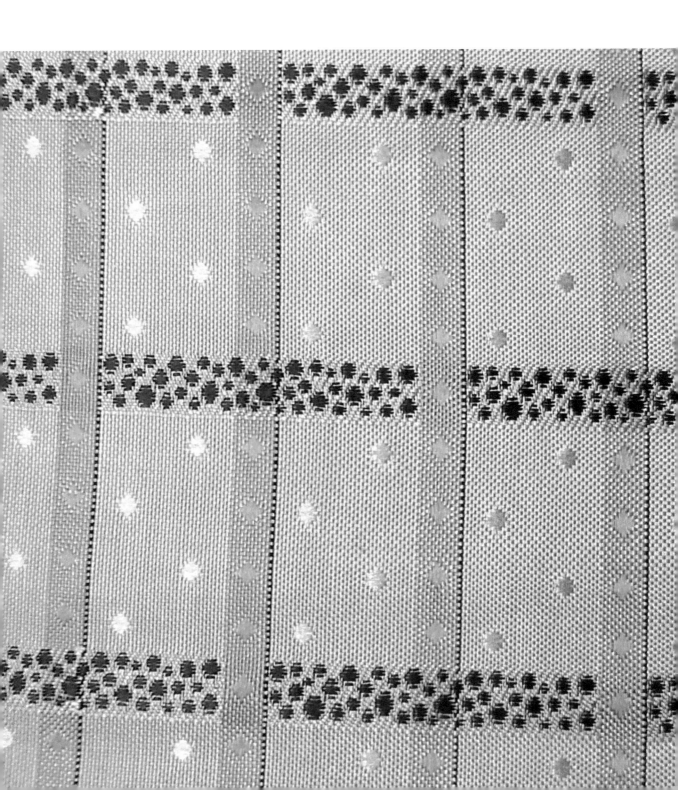

Anonymous for Royal Worcester Porcelain
1940s
Restrained and fragile, this is a delicate watercolour
design of roses, ready for hand-painting application
onto bone china tableware.

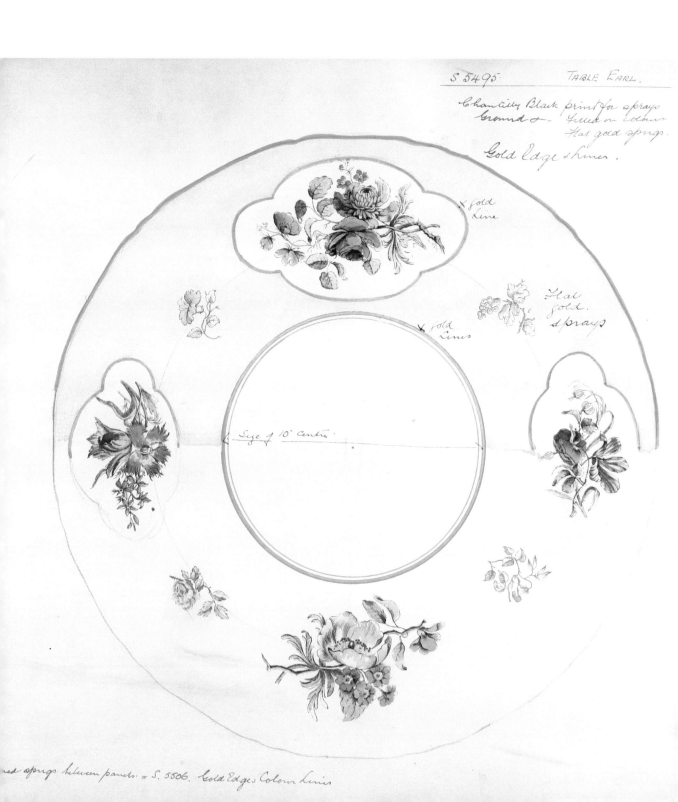

(Probably) Vanessa Bell
Bloomsbury, c.1920s
Freely drawn, this motif of flowers on a background of painterly marks is most probably designed by Vanessa Bell, one of the founders of the Omega Workshops, which was a short-lived but influential artists' co-operative that formed as an offshoot of the Bloomsbury Group.

Anonymous for Royal Worcester Porcelain
1881
This page from a mid 19th-century pattern book
shows how one design could be adapted for
production in a range of different colours.

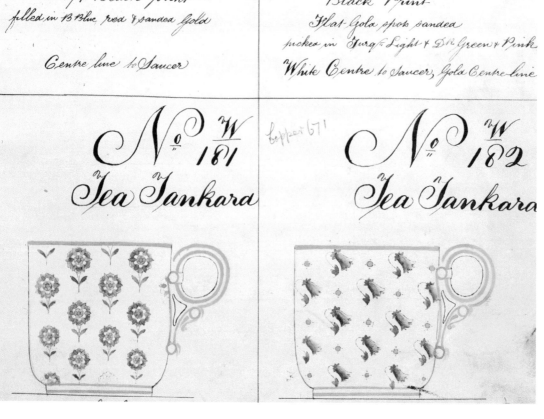

Anonymous
1890s
This spectacular spiral tabletop is a late 19th-century copy of a marquetry Anglo-Sinhalese tabletop, which has been inlaid with radiating veneers of ivory and various coloured native woods. The Galle district of Ceylon (Sri Lanka) was famous for its manufacture of specimen-wood furniture.

Anonymous
1860s
A 'Wearing Blanket' woven by an unknown Native
American artisan, which most probably uses natural
dyes gathered from local plants and minerals to
colour the hand-spun wool.

William De Morgan
c.1870
Designed and made by possibly the most important and innovative ceramic artist of the Arts and Crafts Movement, this panel of sunflowers is in raised relief. De Morgan also designed stained glass and painted furniture but is best known for his ceramic work, which assimilated his experimental glazes and firing techniques.

Charles Rennie Mackintosh
c.1914
Acclaimed Scottish architect, designer and artist,
C. R. Mackintosh experimented with a wide
range of decorative forms, producing designs for
furniture, metalwork and the graphic arts, including
highly stylized posters and pencil and watercolour
textile designs such as this.

Anonymous for John Barlow of Macclesfield
1904
A subtle pink, beige and brown woven silk sample,
probably intended for a muffler or cravat. In the
19th century, the cravat became a fashionable
accessory and thus developed into a basic item
in every gentleman's wardrobe.

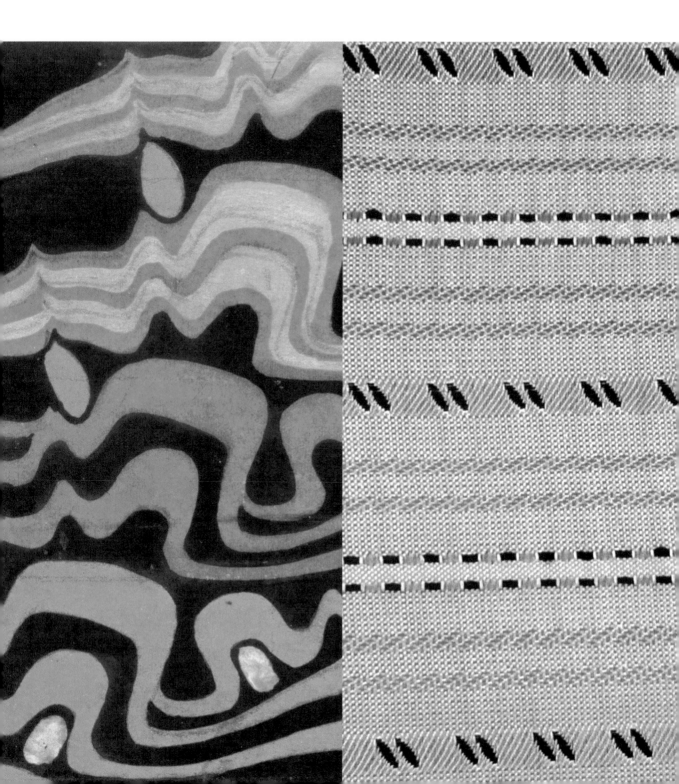

Marie-Noëlle Fontan
2008
This celebrated French artist uses natural materials interwoven with dyed and coloured yarn to create most unusual patterns and designs.

Phyllis Barron and Dorothy Larcher
1920s–30s
Hand block-printed in brown on undyed, hand-woven, Indian cotton, this abstract repeating pattern is another of these artists' understated, rustic designs. Their friend, artist and fellow craftswoman Susan Bosence said of them: 'Their textiles possessed an affinity with the house we were to live in, with its barn foundations, whitewashed stone walls and wooden floors.'

Anonymous
c.1860
Carved from persimmon-soaked mulberry paper, this example of a *katagami*, or Japanese stencil, is a *komon* or small motif stencil. The delicacy of the cutting is extremely skilful, and the laborious and meticulous methods of treating the paper and carving stencils were passed down from master to apprentice over the centuries.

Althea McNish for Liberty of London
Cebollas, 1958
Exotic fruits in subdued colours combine in a
delightful design by this British artist and designer
from Trinidad and Tobago, who became Britain's first
black textile designer of international repute.

Anonymous
c.1890
Originating in the Nara Period (710–94), these *katagami*, or Japanese stencil patterns, were first used for applying designs to leather goods and later came to be used for printing textiles. The jagged shapes on this design imitate a design from the tradition of *itajime* or clamp-resist *shibori* textiles.

Anonymous for Bilbille & Co., Paris
1959–60
Random marks and overlapping brushstrokes give an 'arty' feel to this sample of lacquered and waterproofed acetate, designed for rainwear.

Anonymous
c.1880
This is a detail of an antique *katagami* stencil that was used to produce patterns for kimonos and obis. Traditionally, stencils were cut out of stiff brown paper made from mulberry pulp, then cured and smoked in a preparation process that provided the stencils with moderate water-resistance and strength, as well as giving them their characteristic rich brown colour.

Anonymous
c.1850
A *katagami*, or Japanese hand-cut paper stencil
pattern, used to print textile designs onto lengths
of narrow width cloth. They are made of mulberry
paper saturated with persimmon tannin and are
themselves works of art and highly collectible.

Anonymous
c.1910
This *katagami*, or Japanese paper stencil pattern,
has been cut using the *kiri-bori* method in order to
produce many fine holes. This is extremely intricate
work, requiring great skill and focus.

Anonymous for Langley Printworks
1951–52
A printer's 'fent', or proof on paper, of a quarter design for a hand-printed silk headscarf, showing the frontage of St Paul's Cathedral, London, complete with horse-drawn carriage and tourists.

Reiko Sudo for Nuno Corporation
Walnut, 2008
Combining traditional aesthetics with the latest
computer technology, this innovative Japanese firm
has designed a remarkable dense-piled wool carpet,
based on a pattern of walnut leaves.

Anonymous
1954
Woven depictions of the planet Saturn spinning among the stars are the fascinating subject of this Jacquard rayon brocade sample. Images of outer space and its imagined technology became an overriding fascination for many pattern designers during the 1950s – a decade before space travel became a reality.

Enid Marx
Ashcroft, 1930s
A textile sample that has been dyed with quercitron, a yellow dye obtained from the bark of the eastern black oak, and hand block-printed in chrome red. Incidentally, the notes on the fabric state it as being balloon cotton, but it may in fact be a fine natural linen or even silk, which is what this celebrated artist craftswoman normally used, especially before the Second World War.

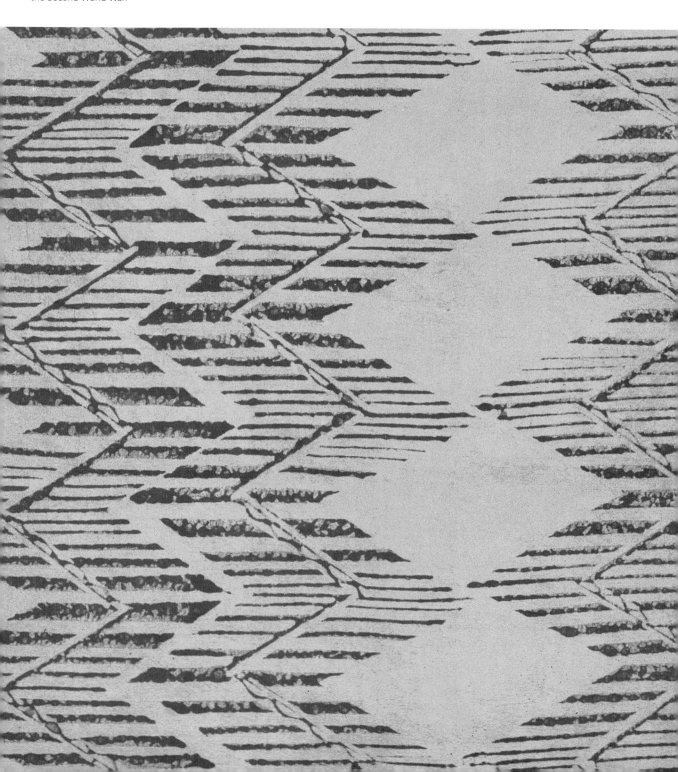

Eric Slater for Shelley Art pottery
Harmony Ware, 1932
Sometimes referred to as 'drip ware', it is said that the idea for this type of pattern was discovered by accident by Eric Slater, who one day mixed too much turpentine with the glaze, making the paint run down the sides of the pot he was decorating. He found the effect interesting and after further experimentation, he created a whole range of *Harmony Ware* for sale.

Anonymous for Bilbille & Co., Paris
1959–60
Produced as a sample for prestigious French
couturier houses, this bold 'tumbling box' pattern
has been screen-printed onto cotton poplin.

Léon Bakst
1909
The celebrated Russian artist and costume designer Léon Bakst created this watercolour design for Stravinsky's *The Firebird* ballet, which was performed by the artistes of Diaghilev's Ballets Russes. Note detail of the textile designs on the skirt and bodice of the dancer; Bakst was a superb pattern designer and his creations were hugely inspirational at the time.

Anonymous for Barracks Printing Co.
1970s
Hand-painted in gouache, this *croquis* for a silk
fashion fabric was intended for Liberty of London.
The unusual design features young ladies in various
states of undress.

Anonymous (American School)
1940s
Drawing largely on mid-European folkloric traditions, this American roller-printed cotton has a pleasant homely quality.

Anonymous for Barracks Printing Co.
1970s
Large full-blown daisies are the chosen motif in this
hand-painted *croquis* design for textiles. The top
left-hand section has been cut out and replaced by
the artist at some point in its creation.

Reiko Sudo for Nuno Corporation
2007
A scattering of little acorn-shaped rounds, woven in pile, adds a note of carefree charm to this wire-cut cotton velvet fabric. It was specially woven in Wakayama, south west Japan, using wires with sharpened ends which are woven in together with the warps; when the wires are pulled out, the blades cut the weft loops and form a velvet pile – a laborious and potentially injurious process.

Anonymous
c.1920
Decorated with a stylized border pattern of oranges
and leaves in black, green and orange, this is a
delightful watercolour design for a teacup. It was
especially difficult to produce a true black glaze at
the very high temperature needed for bone china.
The process was eventually perfected at Worcester
in around 1910.

Reiko Sudo for Nuno Corporation
Broadleaf, 2007
A working drawing inspired by patterns observed in leaves by a Japanese company who specialize in unusual techniques. They comment: 'Nuno works with lesser-known Japanese weaving and dyeing centres to create fabrics that can only be made here and now in Japan. We are especially interested in "earth-friendly" sustainable materials. Who says ecology means boring design?'

Anonymous
Two Quail, 1940s
Revisits of classic Georgian designs were frequently
made over a number of years, as they were so
timeless. This delicate watercolour design is an
adaptation of an oriental pattern first made by
the Worcester Porcelain factory in the 1760s.

William De Morgan
1880s
A beautifully observed portrayal of birds on a foliate background, by this influential Art and Crafts ceramicist. A life-long friend of William Morris, De Morgan designed tiles, stained glass and furniture for Morris & Co. (known as The Firm) from 1863–72. It was then that he rediscovered the technique of using lustre glazes, which give the ceramics an iridescent, metallic surface.

Josef Hoffmann
Serpentin, c.1910–15
Only a rose-coloured background and the insertion
of a tiny hidden heart soften the stark black
geometric shapes in this design for a printed textile.
Josef Hoffmann was a founder member of the
Vienna Secession, the radical forum for avant-garde
artists, designers and architects who wanted to
break with traditional ideas.

Josef Hoffmann
1928
A typically convoluted pattern design on paper
from this master artisan. In 1903, Josef Hoffmann
became co-founder and artistic director of the
Wiener Werkstätte. This multi-disciplinary design
partnership produced handcrafted items including
textiles, jewellery, ceramics and furniture, all
characterized by simple shapes, minimal
decoration and geometric patterning.

Anonymous
1950s
Imitating the hand block prints so popular with printmakers and artists of the era, this is a screen-printed linen curtain fabric made by Heal & Son, featuring stylized birds and flowers.

Enid Marx
Underground, 1930s
This is a hand block-printed textile sample, comprising an abstract design of swirls and loops printed using iron liquor on linen, which results in a dark brown pattern.

Anonymous for John Barlow of Macclesfield
1904
An example of a gentleman's muffler, or scarf, this silk sample is finely woven in carefully modulated shades of brown and olive green.

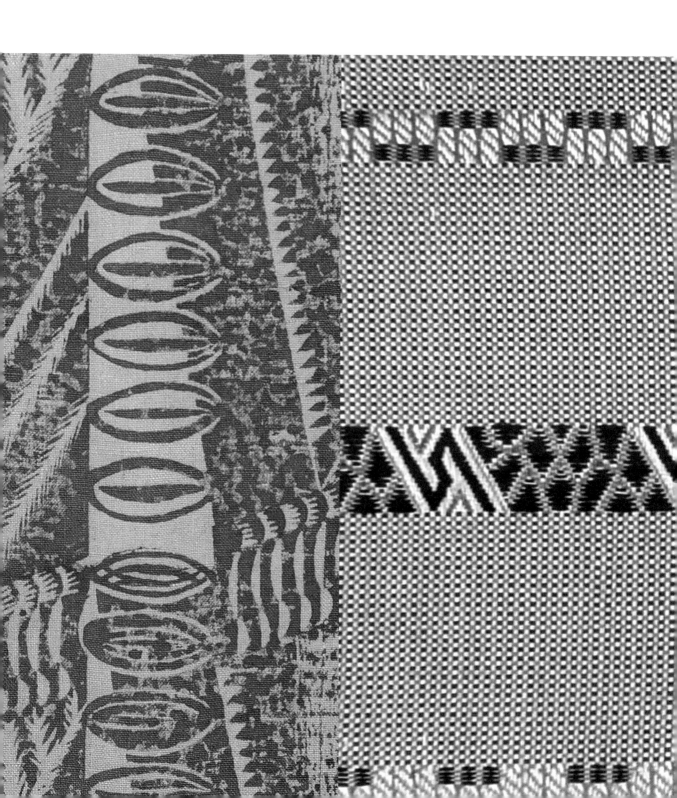

Enid Marx
Woolworth, 1930s
A hand block-printed textile sample, in a criss-cross design of cream on brown, made from cotton dyed in iron liquor and printed with a solution of tin to discharge the design.

Kristina Isola for Marimekko
Metsänväki, 2007
Kristina Isola's fairy-tale *Metsänväki* is dedicated to
dear and faithful friends: to the trees and bushes of
the forest, which stay put year after year.

Eley Kishimoto
2007
Formed by Mark Eley and Wakako Kishimoto in the early 1990s, this design company creates work that is clear in intention, executed simply and with creative flair. This design seems to encapsulate a nostalgic view of the countryside with its hills and dales, trees and hedges.

Susan Bosence
1950s–60s
A deceptively simple pattern of lines, stars and circles cut from linoleum mounted onto wood and hand block-printed onto cotton. In 1950 Susan Bosence visited Phyllis Barron and Dorothy Larcher, the pioneering hand block-printers, and a close relationship developed from there, with Barron giving her encouragement and support in the art of dyeing and printing.

Anonymous
1950s
Originating in Barcelona, Spain, this cheery design of pineapples is arranged in a simple half-drop repeat on a screen-printed furnishing fabric.

Anonymous for Langley Printworks
1951–52
A design featuring naturalistically portrayed birds.
Birds have been used as textile motifs since ancient
times, passing in and out of fashion. By the late
19th century, a growing market for their skins,
bodies and feathers fuelled the killing of hundreds
of thousands of birds. It was not until 1918 that
commercial trade in any migratory bird species or
its feathers was finally outlawed.

Erja Hirvi for Marimekko
Purnukka, 2008
A large-scale furnishing fabric with a pattern
portraying a fascinating array of autumn delicacies
preserved in jars of various shapes. The harvest
in the jars is reflected in the colours of the fabric:
shades of beetroot and pickled gherkin, blueberry
blue and tomato red.

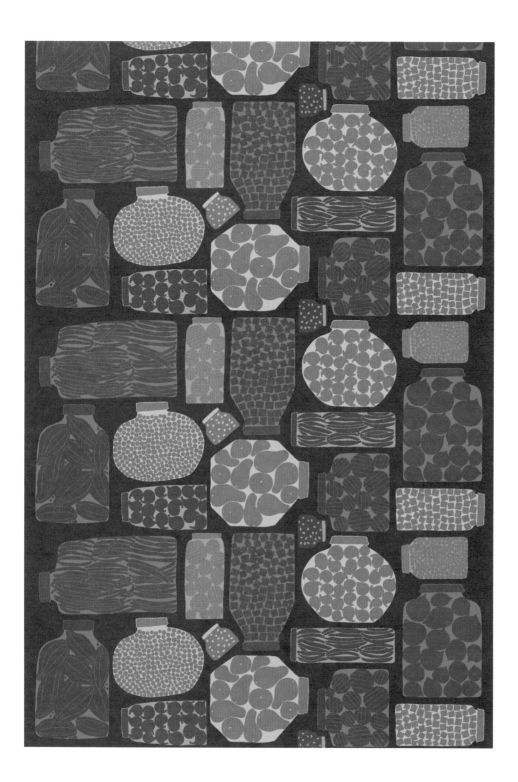

Hannah Firmin
Autumn, 2007
Adroitly produced linocuts have been printed onto different coloured papers by the artist, before she separated and reassembled them into an evocative pastoral design for greeting cards.

Linda Sjunnesson for Spira
Eden, 2006
A melamine-coated tray, printed with an eye-catching pattern of deep red passion flowers and light blue fruits, is just one of the printed products using this design that has been created by this inventive Scandinavian design team.

Anonymous for Barracks Printing Co.
1970s
Images of a large older-style house and two horse chestnut trees, complete with their clusters of pink and white flowers, known as 'candles', decorate this hand-painted *croquis* design for Liberty of London.

(Probably) Duncan Grant

1930s

Printed swags and tails of a theatrical curtain
decorate this furnishing fabric, which was probably
created by the artist Duncan Grant, one of the
founders of the celebrated Omega Workshops,
London, which was in existence from 1913–19,
designing textiles, furniture, ceramics and small
objets d'art for the home.

Anonymous for Bilbille & Co., Paris
1959–60
Dazzling squares of the complementary colours of red and green have been overprinted with a roughly drawn square of black, in this bright silk sample for French fashion houses.

Maija Fagerlund
Keto, 2007
Designed in Finland, this floral pattern of stylized
and silhouetted floral images is digitally manipulated
and printed.

Alexander Girard for máXimo inc.
April, 1960
Simplified outlines of brightly coloured flowers
appear on this screen-printed furnishing fabric,
designed by the distinguished American surface
pattern designer, Alexander Girard.

Anonymous for Barracks Printing Co.
1970s
A dense black background affords maximum
contrast to the exotic flowers portrayed in this
vivid hand-painted *croquis* floral design.

Anonymous
c.1880
A charming pastoral scene of a young couple and
rabbits, surrounded by flowers and featuring a
particularly vibrant red background, upon which the
scene has been superimposed. Pastoral scenes such
as this were popular throughout the 19th century
and represented a rural idyll.

Anonymous for Barracks Printing Co.
1970s
Bold floral designs in shades of orange, peach and beige or brown were very popular in the late 1960s and early 70s. This is a hand-painted *croquis* for dress fabric.

Phyllis Barron and Dorothy Larcher
1930s–40s
A dramatic pattern of bold zigzags, hand block-printed using alizarin, the red colouring compound derived from the root of the madder plant, or *Rubia tinctorum*.

Anonymous
c.1900
Woven in sections of plain dyed yarn interspersed with weft *ikat* yarn, this textile uses unusual fibres, such as coir from the coconut palm, in its construction. *Ikat* is a dyeing technique in which the yarn is tie-dyed before it is woven.

Anonymous
1930s
Striped silk fabric, sometimes referred to as 'Macclesfield Stripe', became very popular in the inter-war years, and was used extensively for blouses, dresses and scarves as well as handkerchiefs of all sizes.

Nicola Wood for Textra Ltd
Everglade, 1972
This combines elements referenced from Japanese
and Chinese textiles with the pop art flowers and
overblown motifs of the period, in a screen-printed
cotton fabric.

Anonymous for F. Steiner & Co.
1903
Rendered in typical Art Nouveau style, this bold water lily design on roller-printed cotton is by a manufacturing company who bought textile designs from leading British freelance designers, as well as from France and Belgium, where the vogue for Art Nouveau patterns was especially strong.

Aino-Maija Metsola for Marimekko
Joiku, 2008
This design for furnishing fabric conveys a powerful
yet calm experience of nature. The pattern shows
the simple beauty of a pure landscape with a
multitude of colours, in the evening dusk or on
a misty morning just before sunrise.

Minä Perhonen
2008
This innovative Japanese fashion house has created a charming cut Jacquard weave for its fashions. The designer comments: 'Strongly alive flowers appear in winter time. Flowers lift up their faces out of a snowy field.'

174

Anonymous
1878
A hand-painted watercolour design for tableware, which has been taken from a pattern book of the late 19th century. The style of drawing and colouration of the birds, butterflies and flowers show the influence of *Chinoiserie*, or Chinese-inspired patterns, on designers in the West.

Gunta Stölzl
1924
A watercolour pen, ink, and pencil design for a textile, executed on paper by this important German master weaver. Stölzl played a pivotal role in the Bauhaus School after becoming the school's weaving director in 1925, applying experimental ideas and initiating innovations to the textile department. Under her direction, the Bauhaus weaving workshop became one of its most successful facilities.

Anonymous for Bilbille & Co., Paris
1959–60
Red flowers and twisted ribbons make a striking
pattern, which has been hand screen-printed onto
cotton poplin in Italy for a Parisian sampling house.

Anonymous
1960s
A mass-produced tablecloth, screen-printed with a floral design onto a rather coarse cotton fabric, although the texture of the cloth does complement the boldness of the imagery.

Anonymous
1930s–40s
Orange and brown butterflies crowd into the corner of this hand block-printed rayon handkerchief. Rayon, or 'artificial silk', had become the fibre of choice for the majority of ladies fashion fabrics at this time, being affordable and easy to wash and iron, as well as being pleasant to look at and wear.

Rachel Goodchild
Red Roses, 2008
Achieved by means of collage and digital manipulation, this red rose pattern echoes similar designs by Richard Riemerschmid and others, including Paul Poiret, the celebrated French fashion designer of the early 20th century, who made a highly stylized rose into his personal emblem.

Anonymous for Langley Printworks
1935–39
A printer's 'fent', or test on paper, this quarter design for a headscarf seems to be somewhat out of its correct registration. Nonetheless, it does have a forthright and appealing quality to it.

Drusilla Cole
1999
A hand-printed pattern derived from an original linocut, subsequently digitally manipulated into repeat. The inspiration was the rich area of European folkloric tradition.

Ella Doran
2008
Spotted grey ribbons zigzag their way across a cheerful digitally printed design for gift wrap. Spotty patterns are always in fashion it seems.

Sergi Petrovitch Burylin
Tractor, 1930
Roller-printed onto cotton by the Ivanovo-
Voznesensk textile mill, Russia, this dazzling design
was produced to promote the country's newly
mechanized agriculture in accordance with Soviet
dictates of the time.

Tricia Guild and Kaffe Fassett
Leaf Layers, 1978
A lively screen-printed wallpaper produced for
the Designers Guild, by these two exceptional
artists. Tricia Guild founded the Designers Guild in
the 1970s, which is characterized by its striking
patterns and dramatic and courageous use of
colour. Kaffe Fassett is an American artist, well
known for his colourful designs in every area of
decorative textile design.

Anonymous for Barracks Printing Co.
1970s
A delightful bunch of fresh flowers has been loosely
rendered in watercolour and gouache in this *croquis*
for fashion fabrics.

Darya Preobrazhenskaya
Skaters, 1927–30
An uplifting Soviet textile produced in the 'thematic' style of design. This style involved the use of geometric, symbolic and propaganda motifs. The designs themselves were fairly simple and lively, often with an industrial theme to them and were a form of popular visual propaganda that could be easily understood and interpreted.

Florence Broadhurst
1963–77
Possibly inspired by ancient Chinese designs and motifs, this geometric design for hand-printed wallpaper was designed by an eccentric Australian artist and entrepreneur.

Anonymous for Bilbille & Co., Paris
1959–60
Wool serge, which is a hard-wearing twill weave with good draping qualities, has been screen-printed with a leafy design in autumnal colours.

S. M. Slade for British Celanese Ltd
1951
Based on the crystal structure diagram of afwillite,
this is a sample of a screen-printed spun rayon
dress fabric. The designs are interpretations of the
atomic structures, yet they are also scientifically
accurate. This was a completely new source of
inspiration for the designers; a rich field of natural
pattern designs.

Enid Seeney for Ridgeway Potteries Ltd
Homemaker, 1955
Decorated with iconic images of contemporary British design, such as a boomerang-shaped table, a spindly-legged plant pot and an 'art' lamp, this design has become a classic of its kind. It was mass-produced for sale through Woolworth in Britain, and had a long production run.

Lucienne Day for Arthur Sanderson and Sons
1953
A screen-printed furnishing fabric featuring the
distinctive variety of marks and carefully placed
blocks of colours that characterize this important
designer's post-war textile designs.

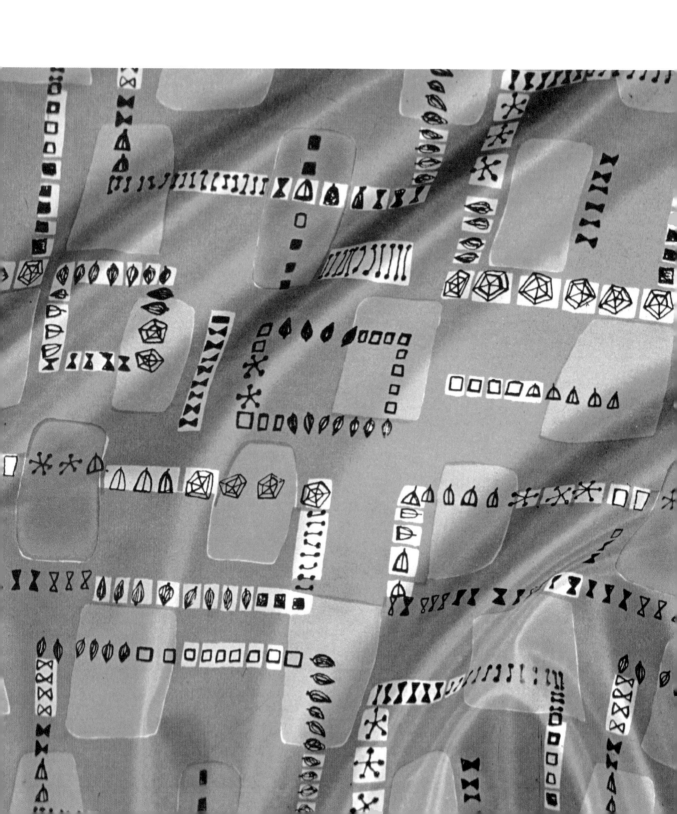

Alice Archer
Millefleur, 2007
Featuring digital and domestic machine embroidery, this design couples the familiar with the strange. The artist comments: 'My inspiration came from the decorative flora and fauna of archaic tapestries, in particular the *Lady and the Unicorn* tapestries of the Museé National du Moyen Age, Paris.'

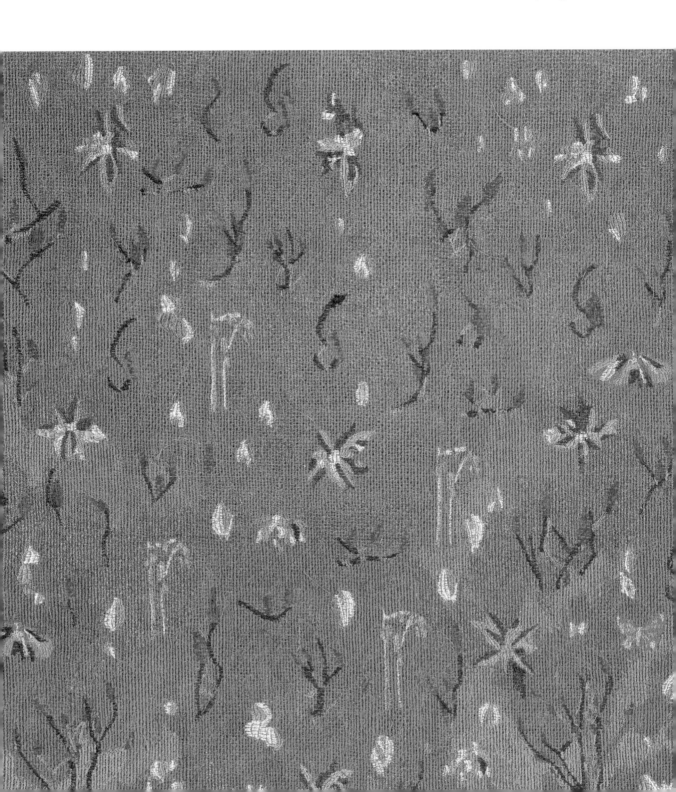

Drusilla Cole
2008
An antique *katagami* stencil has been digitally manipulated to create its design. The traditional process of printing, called *katazome*, relied on a sticky rice paste being pressed through the stencil to act as a resist. Once dyed, the resist paste was washed off the fabric and the finished design would be revealed.

Eley Kishimoto
Birdy, 2003
Mark Eley and Wakako Kishimoto are a highly acclaimed design partnership whose work has become synonymous with their distinctive graphic prints and patterns.

Anonymous for Brocklehurst Whiston Amalgamated

1947

A stirring hand-painted design of ocean-going yachts with their sails set and all hands on deck makes for an unusual fabric design. On the design can be seen the faint pencilled outline of squares, which would be needed to prepare the pattern for the loom.

Anonymous
1950s
Vignettes of floral images are linked by curving lines
in a hand screen-printed cotton fabric for curtains.
The white lines allow for easy registration – a bonus
when screen printing.

Anonymous
c.1880
Based on the design of a patchwork quilt, in fact
this French Indiennes fabric is an interpretation of
Indian hand-printed cottons. The cleverly applied
printed lines of stitching on the fabric help augment
the impression that it is a quilted piece.

Anonymous
1930s
A bold design in red, green and blue, which, with its
forthright and decisive brushstrokes, is reminiscent
of the style of Vanessa Bell, the eminent artist and
intellectual of the early 20th century.

Anonymous
c.1890
A pretty roller-printed fabric, originating from
France, which has a complex floral pattern derived
from the Indian chintzes prevalent at the time.

Anonymous
1930s–40s
Mistletoe and colourful berries have been painted in
gouache on paper, perhaps as a Christmas novelty
pattern. Mistletoe is a rather mysterious plant
parasite with a complex folklore. It has been used
as a popular motif for many years, especially for
Art Nouveau designs of the early 20th century.

Duncan Grant for Allan Walton Textiles
1936
Produced for furnishings for the first-class lounge of the *Queen Mary* liner, this large semi-abstract design was, alas, never used. Duncan Grant was a prominent member of the Bloomsbury Group and co-director of the Omega Workshops, London, as well as being a sensitive painter and designer.

Anonymous
1950s
Brilliant red colouring was widely used in the post-
war period, doubtless as a way of heartening the
spirits after the privations of earlier times. Thrusting
patterns of young plant growth were also popular
– probably for the same reasons.

Anonymous for Langley Printworks
1935–39
Multicoloured balls crowd around the centre of
this printer's 'fent', or proof on paper, for this hand
block-printed design for a large handkerchief.

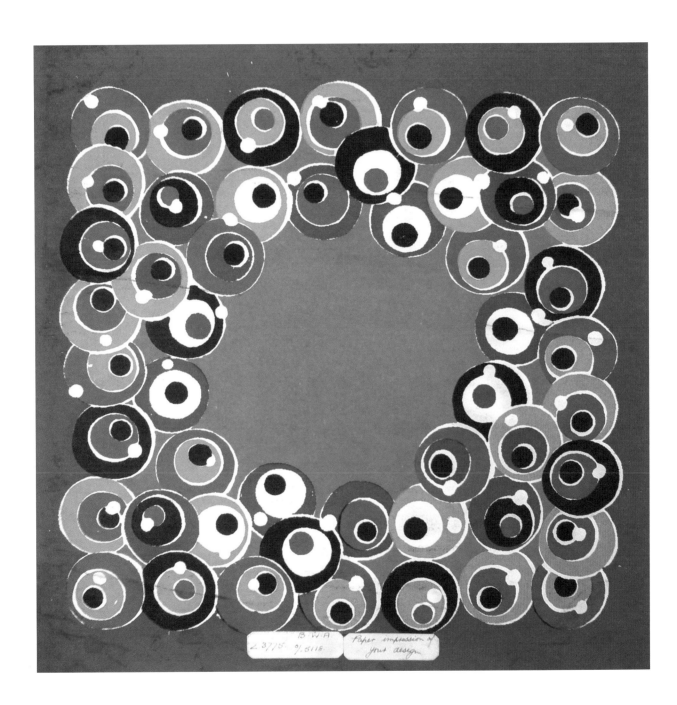

Anonymous for Burleigh Ware
1950s
Tiny grey tassels surmounted with red dots
surround a bright red inner circle. Brilliant red
colours are notoriously difficult to achieve in
ceramics, as they need a lead glaze – a highly toxic
substance. This was in use in the 1950s, before
rigorous health and safety rules were introduced.

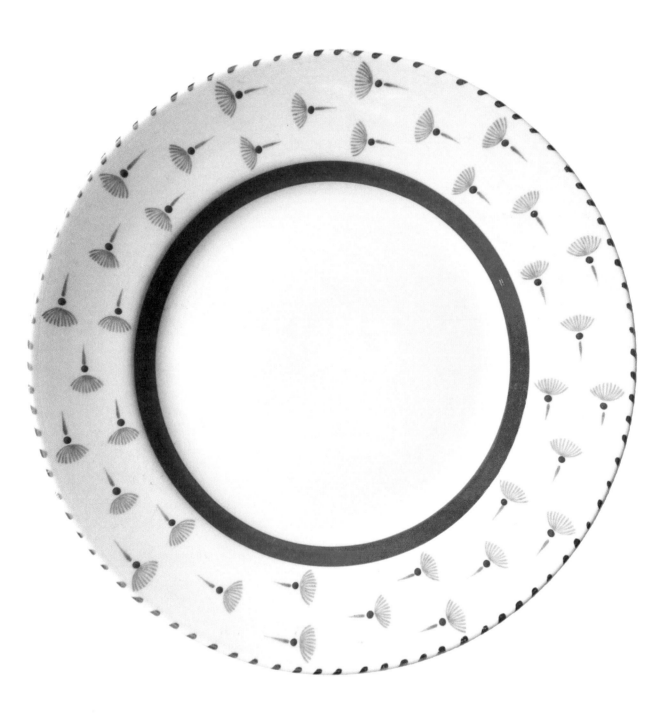

Anonymous
1950s
Kitchen utensils were popular as motifs in the 1950s, probably because kitchens themselves included a newly redesigned décor and appliances such as refrigerators, toasters and stoves.

Anonymous for John Barlow of Macclesfield
1904
The popularity of Japanism began in the mid 19th
century, just after Japanese trade with the West
was opened, and lasted for the next 60 years or
so in France and England. All manner of objets d'art
were influenced by Japanese designs, including this
woven silk sample for a waistcoat or cravat.

Phyllis Barron and Dorothy Larcher
1920s–30s
In 1925, a young artist, Enid Marx, joined these indomitable craftswomen for a year. As she recalled, it was challenging work: '...dyeing and all the preparations... Moreover, steaming and washing, an onerous job before the washing machine, when everything had to be washed and rinsed a number of times by hand, much of it hosed down out of doors. Then there was ironing galore...'.

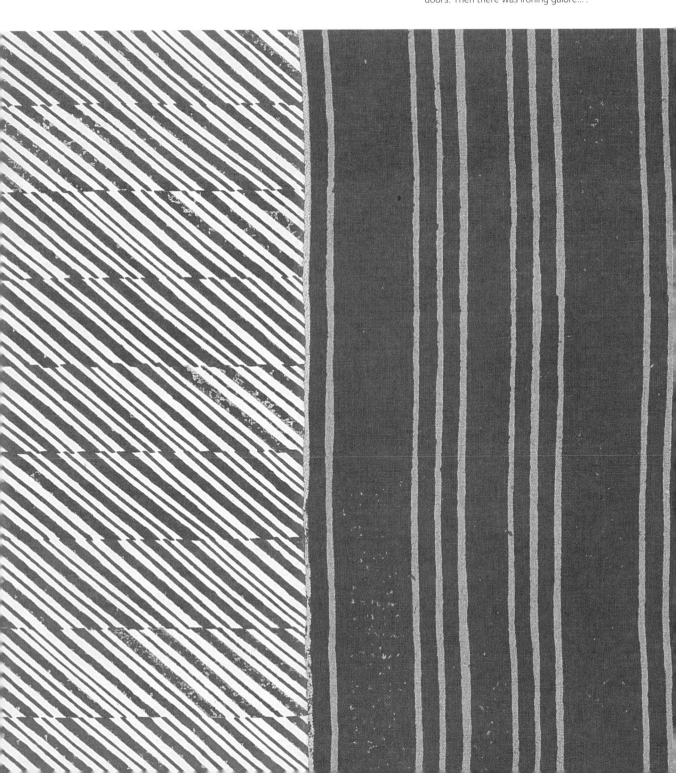

Anonymous
c.1880
Chinese auspicious characters and motifs for long
life and happiness have been incorporated into
the pattern of this length of multicoloured woven
silk fabric.

Anonymous
c.1880
French mill-engraved cotton printed using the dye
madder. Madder is obtained from the root of the
Rubia tinctorum and has been in use since ancient
times. It is extremely useful as a dye as it can
produce a wide range of hues – reds, rusts, oranges,
browns and purples, depending upon the technique
employed. It was the most commonly used dye in
the 18th and 19th centuries for everyday clothing.

Anonymous for Barracks Printing Co.
1970s
Produced as a *croquis* for Berne Silks, this hand-painted gouache geometric design may have been inspired by overlapping filmstrips, a spooled strip of 35mm film with images arranged sequentially.

Anonymous for J & T Brocklehurst
c.1850
A Jacquard woven ladies dress fabric which includes a very lifelike piece of black lace – actually a *trompe l'oeil* part of the weave. Fashions of the time had a number of flounces, edged with embroidery or velvet bands. As the decade progressed, evening dresses were trimmed with more and more ruches, puffs, ribbons, flounces and lace.

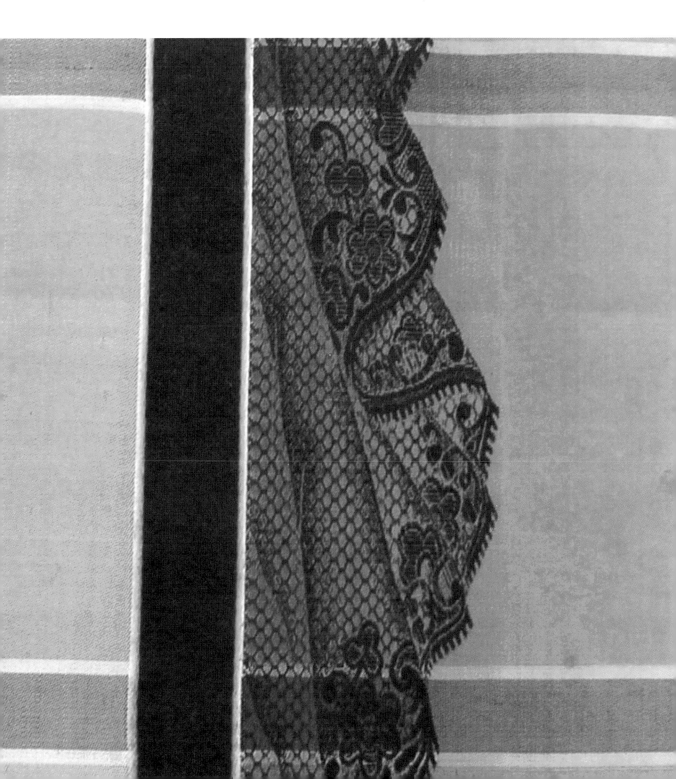

Anonymous for Bilbille & Co., Paris
1959–60
Sweeping lines in black and magenta cover this
lacquered and waterproofed printed acetate
sample intended for couture rainwear.

Anonymous for Bilbille & Co., Paris
1959–60
Mysterious and intense, this hand screen-printed
Italian silk sample would have been offered to top
Parisian couturier houses such as Christian Dior.

Anonymous
1940s
Roller-printed onto acetate rayon, this design of roses and silhouetted leaves was an affordable substitute for silk for women who were eager to purchase the newest designs and colour-ways at an economical price.

l Goodchild

Autumn Leaves, 2006
Carefully cut and collaged oak leaf and acorn shapes in harmonious autumnal shades are scattered over this design for gift wrap and evoke the feeling of a blustery fall day.

Anonymous for Barracks Printing Co.
1960s
A hand-painted *croquis* for fashion fabrics, which incorporates adaptations of the paisley or Indian *boteh* motif. The ultra-bright or 'psychedelic' colours and Indian patterns were widespread during this era, appearing on all manner of surface patterns, from headscarves to wallpaper.

Anonymous
c.1890
A detail of a delicately shaded, vintage silk kimono fabric, which uses the *Yuzen* resist dyeing technique, whereby a paste mixture is used to draw motifs on white silk, before the artist paints the areas using the desired dye colours. The dots and tiny circles in the foreground have been created by a hand-binding technique called *ne-make shibori*.

Anonymous for Langley Printworks
1922–25
Brightly coloured rows of stylized flowers form the design on this sample of a hand block-printed silk taken from a pattern book dating from the 1920s. Textile pattern books contain pages of snippets of printed or woven fabrics, some of which only exist as samples, others of which were in full production.

Anonymous for Barracks Printing Co.
1960s
Daisies were the quintessential symbol of the
1960s and appeared on every possible surface,
from cushions to kaftans. In this *croquis* for
a fashion fabric, they were hand-painted in
gouache and ink.

Samantha Doe
2007
Shown is the artist's first rug design. She comments:
'The design came about through colour proportion
samples inspired by Mark Rothko's work. I was
working from tropical flowers and the lily had
turned to a lovely deep turquoise-purple colour, and
I knew it would stand out against orange... I entered
a "Design-A-Rug" competition with the design and
came second.'

Jessie Tait for Midwinter Pottery
Domino, 1956
A hand-painted border in bright red with alternating spots of white decorates this ceramic plate, which became one of Midwinter's most iconic designs.

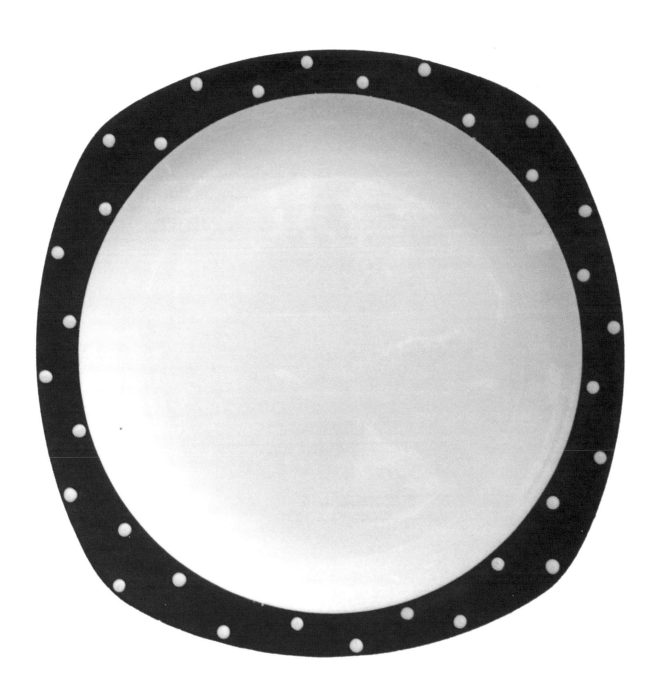

Hennie Haworth
2007
An illustration by a prolific freelance designer, this
digitally manipulated repeat pattern for gift wrap
and greeting cards is likely to be a favourite with
sweet-toothed people everywhere.

Ella Doran
2003
A photograph of a tangled heap of tennis shoes has been carefully digitally manipulated into a repeat design for gift wrap.

Tricia Guild and Kaffe Fassett
Pebbledash, 1978
A single colour wallpaper from the *Geranium*
collection designed by these two eminent designers
for Tricia Guild's company, the Designers Guild.

Diana Low
1920s–30s
Deceptively simple flower shapes and fine wavy
lines decorate this rose-pink screen-printed
furnishing fabric.

Tobie Jennings
2007
A mixed-media design on silk, created using a digital print overlaid with hand-printing and painting. The novels of Thomas Hardy, principally *Tess of the D'Urbervilles*, were the inspiration for this artist. She comments: 'The images are the ribbons of the maypole and wild flower garlands. The roses represent the controlled symbol of nature.'

Henry Moore
Three Standing Figures, c.1944
Closely related to this famous sculptor's drawings
for his massive sculptures, this hand screen-printed
scarf was produced by Zika and Lida Ascher who
had invited several prominent artists and designers
to create patterns for silk squares, which were to be
manufactured by their small textile company. The
designs were launched in New York and London and
proved very popular, winning accolades worldwide.

Anonymous
c.1885
An example of a mill-engraved, roller-printed, cotton textile from France. Around 1810, a way was devised of mill-engraving a steel printing roller with small repeating designs. This method was then widely used in the last half of the 19th century to produce fabric printed with fine lines and elaborate, minute patterns.

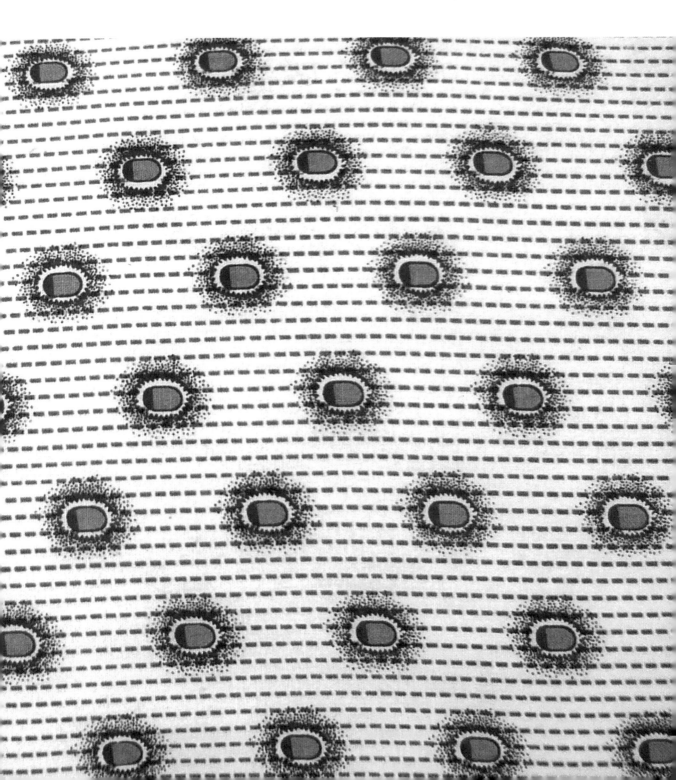

Anonymous
c.1900
Woven details based on the patterns of card suits
– hearts, clubs, diamonds and hearts form the
unusual pattern on this silk sample woven in Spain.

Anonymous
c.1920
Regular shapes in grey and cream are interspersed
with small black squares on this Spanish Jacquard
woven silk sample intended for fashion fabrics.

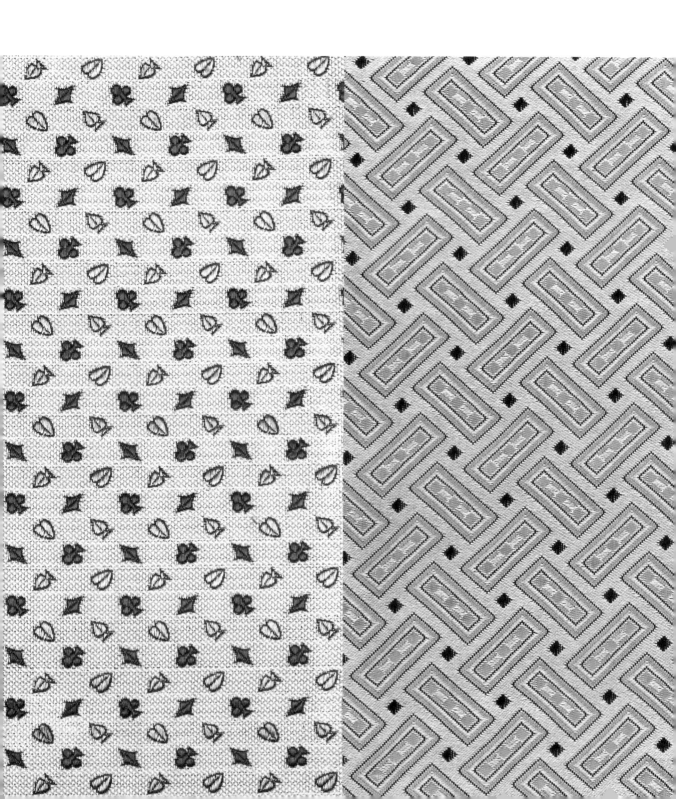

Anonymous (French School)
c.1945
In textiles, ethnic or folk-inspired designs are referred to as 'folkloric' designs, as in this roller-printed example. Here, stylized flowers surround falling figures dressed in traditional costume.

Anonymous for Barracks Printing Co.
1960s
Flower power was the big design movement in this
decade, producing floral images for every surface
pattern opportunity. This example is a hand-painted
croquis for a dress fabric manufacturer.

Duncan Grant
Grapes, 1932
A large-scale furnishing fabric by Duncan Grant, who, in addition to being a textile designer, was also a skilled painter, illustrator, printmaker and commercial interior decorator.

Henry Moore
Piano, 1947
Hand screen-printed onto wool by Ascher Textiles,
a small textile production company, this celebrated
sculptor's textile design uses an enigmatic pattern
of horizontal bands of piano keys, clock faces and
hands extended across the fabric.

Henry Moore
Reclining Figures, 1944–46
The famous sculptor Henry Moore's characteristic emphasis on the mass and form of the figure is translated admirably onto cloth by textile manufacturer Zika Ascher's groundbreaking approach to screen-printing. In this instance, Ascher used a discharge technique to capture the texture and subtlety of Moore's original drawings.

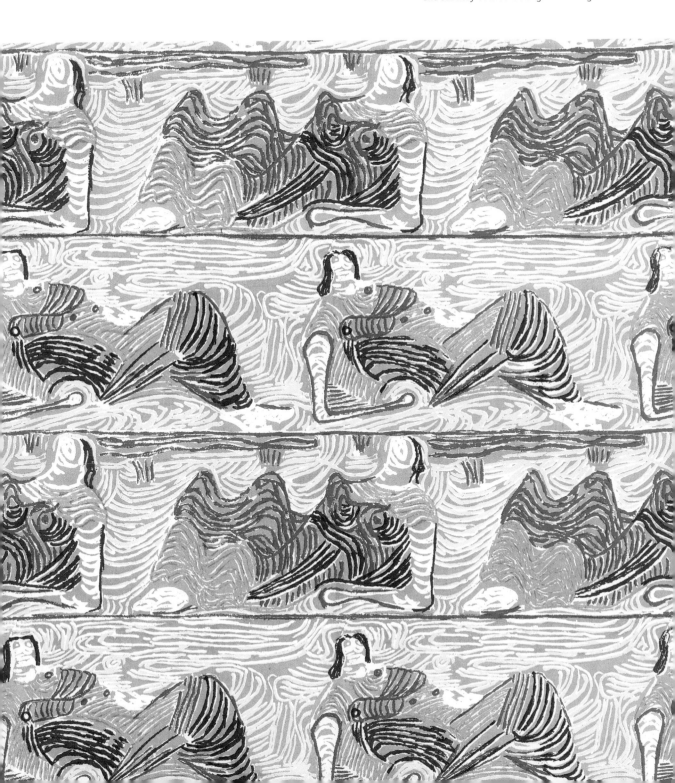

Anonymous for Langley Printworks
1900–12
A printer's 'fent', or proof on paper, of a delightful
floral design for hand block-printed silk that was
intended as a border pattern for dresses.

Drusilla Cole
2003
Comprising discharge-prints and positive prints onto hand-dyed grey silk, this pattern features a mêlée of rock 'n' roll dancers. The artist comments: 'This pattern was one I first designed when I was into airbrushing back in the 1980s. I photocopied my original painting and used different sized images of it to make a small silkscreen, which I printed across the dyed fabric.'

Anonymous
1920s–30s
Roller-printed onto cotton, this leaf-patterned fabric has been used to make a quilt, hence the vertical white stitching lines. The bright magenta leaves add a dynamic enlivening quality to the pattern, which might otherwise have been rather dull.

Ella Doran
2008
Representing joy and longevity in ancient Asian art, these multicoloured butterflies have been digitally manipulated into an attractive and auspicious pattern for gift wrap.

Michael O'Connell
Torro, c.1939
Doubtless inspired by visits to Spain and the Mediterranean coast, this is a hand screen-printed cotton furnishing fabric produced by Edinburgh Weavers. This firm embraced screen printing, a relatively new technique at the time, and commissioned original designs from innovative Modernist avant-garde artist-designers, including sculptor Barbara Hepworth and painter John Piper.

Josef Hoffmann
Kiebitz, 1910–13
A six-colour hand wood-block print on linen
designed for the Wiener Werkstätte, of which
Hoffmann was co-founder and artistic director.
Geometric designs, economy of ornament and
disciplined colour awareness characterized his
designs for surface patterns.

Anonymous
Down with Illiteracy, 1927–31
A roller-printed cotton dress fabric with what was termed a 'new theme', produced for the Soviet Republics of Central Asia. The pattern on this fabric includes figures of women wearing headscarves who are working on a production line of some sort. It uses jagged and energetic shapes to emphasize their industry.

Anonymous (French School)
1933
A paper impression of a sharply angular textile design originating in France, which is very much in the Art Deco style. Discordant vertical shapes were popular throughout the late 1920s and early 30s.

Anonymous for Bilbille & Co., Paris
1959–60
Screen-printed onto acetate satin, this French fabric
sample features purple and yellow anemones and
roses, which have been set out in an open, trailing
lattice-style pattern.

Henry Moore
Insect Wings and Ovals, c.1947
Hand screen-printed in an unusual and striking
colour combination of purple and chartreuse green,
this lively and surprising pattern comprises ovals
and shapes derived from insect wings. Henry
Moore's textiles, as well as his famous sculptures,
have the ability to excite and demand attention.

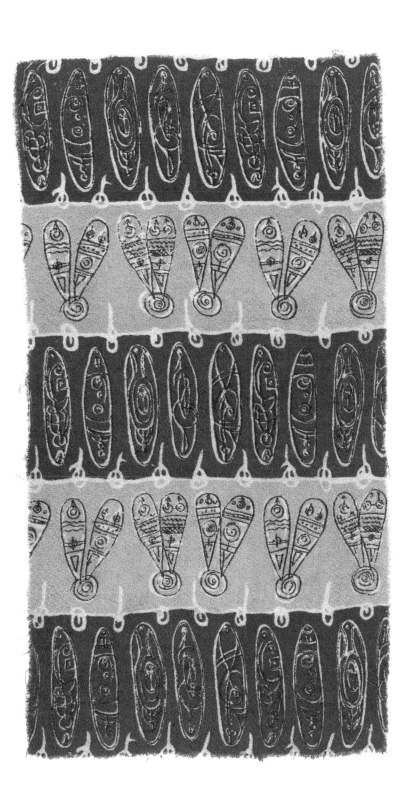

Anonymous
1930s
Gouache painted in rich intense colours, this *croquis* pattern of old-fashioned spinning-tops is a French design for children's wear. The top is one of the oldest recognizable toys found on archaeological sites. It also makes a visually exciting motif.

Anonymous for the Old Bleach Linen Co.
Penguin, 1936
Hand block-printed linen, featuring a pattern of lovable penguins. These were introduced to London Zoo in 1934, when pioneer architect Berthold Lubetkin's Tecton firm designed the Penguin Pool, an acknowledged masterpiece of Modernist design. Interestingly, the Penguin Pool is no longer considered suitable for penguins, so the birds have been moved to a pool elsewhere in the zoo.

Minä Perhonen
1997
Lovely little mauve berries on sprigs have been machine-embroidered all over an enchanting fashion fabric, designed by this innovative Japanese firm.

Ella Doran
2008
Rows of glittering sandals are expertly photographed and digitally manipulated by this enterprising and versatile designer, in order to create a repeating pattern for gift wrap.

Anonymous
1930s–40s
Roller-printed onto acetate rayon, this design would
be printed as a full-width fabric, before being cut up
and made into handkerchiefs. 'Cut-ups' for scarves,
handkerchiefs and ties were the staple product of
many printworks.

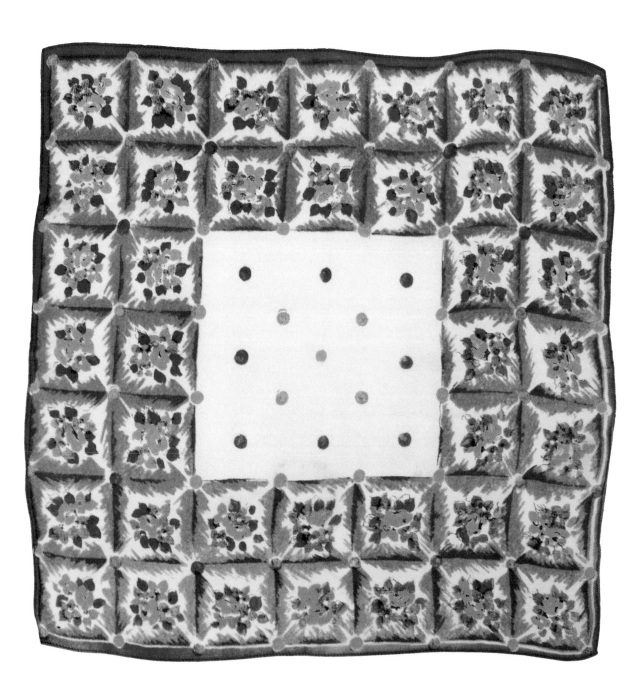

Anonymous for Royal Tudor Ware
Rosalie, 1950s
A transfer-printed pattern of long-stemmed roses
has been hand-painted with yellows and mauves
on this large serving plate, which was influenced
by the contemporary 'organic Modernism' style
of domestic tableware.

Madame de Andrada for Paul Dumas
1925
Hand block-printed cotton in the fashionable Cubist style of the 1920s, whereby forms were portrayed using geometric shapes such as the cone, cylinder and sphere. Paul Dumas was a block-printing manufacturer, who produced the wallpapers for the celebrated couturier, Paul Poiret.

Kim Barnett
2006
This avant-garde freelance designer has digitally enhanced and repeated flowers constructed out of wire, which are repeated horizontally to make a surreal motif for a textile.

Cole and Son (Wallpapers) Ltd
Canonbury, 2007
Drawing on a unique archive of original drawings and wallpapers from the last three centuries, Cole and Son's designs are carefully selected and adapted by their design studio and printed by artisans to produce wallpapers that are faithful to the character of the original document, yet contemporary in ambience. A silk damask from 1750 inspired this fine wallpaper, entitled *Canonbury*.

Maija Isola for Marimekko
Unikko, 1964
An iconic flower pattern that was first created in
the 1960s. Over the years it has been adapted,
recoloured and refined, and today it is probably
more popular than ever, with a countless number
of *Unikko* variations and products available.

244

Raisa Matveeva
1927
Produced in the large Ivanovo-Voznesensk mills,
Russia, this complex and dynamic repeating pattern
of small early aeroplanes is roller-printed onto
cotton. It was sold all over the Soviet Union as a
way of bringing political propaganda to its citizens.

(Probably) Darya Preobrazhenskaya
1927–31
Tractors were a favourite motif of Soviet propaganda textiles, exemplifying progress in agriculture and the vision of the communist future that belonged to the workers.

Anonymous
1930s
Conspicuously coloured in bright yellow, magenta
and blue, these naturalistic representations of
flowers and leaves are gracefully arranged around
the edges of a roller-printed ladies silk handkerchief.

Hennie Haworth
2007
Featuring the once ubiquitous red Routemaster bus, so beloved of London commuters and tourists alike, this digital design for greeting cards and gift wrap also includes a varied assortment of other modes of transport.

Anonymous
1950s
The log cabin quilt pattern has been an established
favourite for many years due to the simplicity of
its design, as well as its value in using up scraps of
fabric. The overall effect of the design is achieved
by the use of light and dark fabrics and how they
are arranged.

Anonymous
c.1930
Vivid blocks of colour vie for attention in this
dynamic and unusual hand-printed handkerchief.
Screen printing began commercially in Britain in
around 1930, with hand block-printing still in use
until the late 1940s, when it became reserved
mainly for top-end printing on silk.

Vanessa Bell for Foley China
c.1934
An impressive bone china plate decorated by
Vanessa Bell, a well-known painter and designer of
the early 20th century, who was commissioned by
Foley China as part of an initiative to use designs
by leading avant-garde artists of the day.

Anonymous
1890s
Roller-printed using madder, this detail of a
patchwork quilt is stitched in white, using
a herringbone pattern. This piece of fabric has
a variegated line pattern, sometimes referred
to as *vermicelli*, or 'little worm', design.

Anonymous for Barracks Printing Co.
1970s
A lazy daisy is painted in gouache as a *croquis* for a fashion fabric. Without the computer technology that designers use now, a mistake meant a section of the design had to be physically removed and replaced – as in the bottom left-hand corner of this example.

Aino-Maija Metsola for Marimekko
Terttu, 2008
An original watercolour of autumnal rowanberries and leaves is admirably translated into a bold and evocative design for furnishing fabrics, which is produced by this successful Finnish design company.

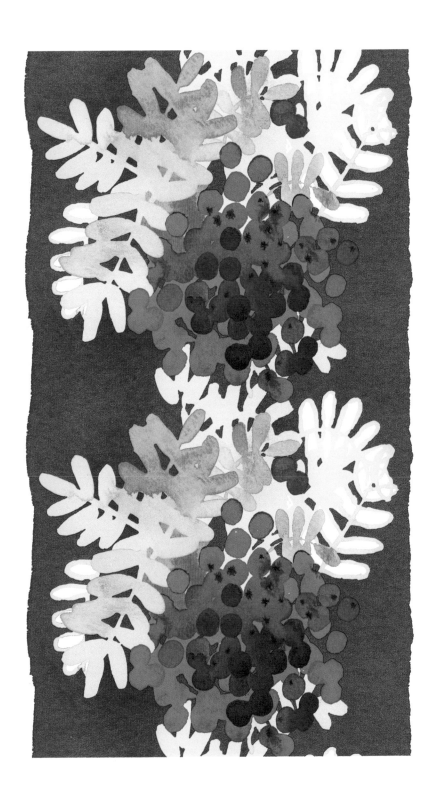

Anonymous
c.1860
Exuberant floral motifs or arabesques pattern this
French fabric, which was hand-woven on a Jacquard
loom using a pleasing array of natural dye colours,
which probably included madder, fustic and indigo.

Anonymous
1950s
Brightly coloured depictions of a butterfly, and the small gentian flowers that surround it, turn this wall plate from Spain into a charming decorative item.

Robert Stewart
1950s
Robert Stewart was a highly notable Scottish artist-
designer in post-war Britain, producing paintings,
tapestries, graphics, ceramics and murals. He also
had a distinguished career in academia, culminating
in his becoming Deputy Director of the Glasgow
School of Art in 1982.

Anonymous
1920s
Superbly hand block-printed in black with numerous tiny multicolour elements, this pattern is part of a top quality silk chiffon scarf.

Anonymous
1950s
Alternating pink and grey slices decorate an
unmarked ceramic plate that probably originates
from Britain in the 1950s.

Anonymous
1870s
A charming design of a ribbon-tied bouquet of flowers has been hand block-printed in madder and pale grey onto linen, for a design that probably originated in France.

Anonymous
1930s–40s
Roses are roller-printed onto rayon acetate, or
'artificial silk', which allowed many women access to
fashionable dress fabrics and accessories for around
half the price of genuine silk products.

Anonymous
1930s
The combination of red, black and white is always popular and is used very effectively on this hand-printed design for a silk handkerchief.

Anonymous for Bilbille & Co., Paris
1959–60
A cleverly constructed textile design of rose-
patterned striped plates has been hand screen-
printed onto cotton poplin as a sample for a Parisian
fashion house.

Anonymous
1930s
Under normal circumstances, French 'ticking', the strong, tightly woven cotton fabric used to make pillow and mattress coverings, is unseen, which would be a pity here, as it is an example of a delightful pattern.

Anonymous for Langley Printworks
1935–39
Graphic representations of flowers have been
illustrated with great care and considerable skill
on this hand block-printed design for scarves.

Anonymous for Bilbille & Co., Paris
1959–60
This bias-cut, acetate satin has been warp-printed with a design of flowers. Warp printing is a long-established technique and gives a soft and subtle edge to this design.

Drusilla Cole
2003
Discharge-printed onto dark grey hand-dyed silk,
this design of roses and leaves was drawn from life
and is designed for use as a fashion fabric.

Anonymous for Barracks Printing Co.
1960s
An appealing design of daisies has been painted
and pieced together in a *croquis* design for fashion
fabrics. The small irregular lines on the design
correspond to areas that have been removed
and replaced by the designer, probably to rectify
an error.

Henry Moore
Four Standing Figures and One Reclining Figure,
1945–46
A mono-printed silk fabric by this outstanding
British sculptor, whose design of elegantly
depicted motifs recalls classical Greek statues
and architecture.

Alice Stevenson for St Judes
Treehouse, 2008
Abstract images resembling mobiles or fluttering flags, these motifs have been screen-printed in two colours onto linen, for a contemporary variation of a 1950s textile design. The artist-designer is one of an eclectic number who produce printed designs for this young company based in Norfolk, England.

Anonymous for Bilbille & Co., Paris
1959–60
Smart and sophisticated patterns of geometric shapes and black brushstrokes have been screen-printed onto pure silk twill for this fashion sample for Parisian couturiers.

Anonymous for Bilbille & Co., Paris
1959–60
A luxurious sample of silver stylized roses screen-printed onto black velvet, this sample was probably intended for ladies evening wear.

Enid Marx
1930s
A textile sample made from cotton, which has been hand block-printed in iron liquor and dark red using simple plant motifs. Enid Marx was an enterprising artist-designer who also worked as a printmaker, painter, children's book author and illustrator, and designer of book jackets, trademarks and postage stamps. In 1937, she was commissioned to design woven seating fabric for London Underground trains.

Angelo Testa
Campagna, 1951
A furnishing fabric, designed by one of Chicago's
most prominent 20th-century designers, whose
abstract geometric and minimalist patterns were
revolutionary for their time. He sold his own screen-
printed textiles and produced designs for major
manufacturers such as Knoll, who reintroduced
Campagna in 1997 in celebration of Knoll Textiles'
fiftieth anniversary.

Anonymous for Langley Printworks
1951–52
One of the lions from Trafalgar Square, London, is set against the imposing structure of the National Gallery, in this section of an evocative hand screen-printed design for a square headscarf.

Anonymous for Langley Printworks
1951–52
A quarter of a design featuring a vivacious sketch
of Buckingham Palace, London, on a scarf designed
for the tourist market. These types of scarves were
often distributed abroad by large export houses.

Dorothy Larcher
Basket, 1920s
A hand block-printed length of unbleached linen, with a positive print in black, printed using a wood-block cut by Dorothy Larcher. *Basket* was an especially popular design, frequently used for curtaining, and although it was only the third block that Larcher had ever cut, it continued to be printed throughout the 1930s.

Angie Lewin
2008
A two-colour design screen-printed onto heavy-
weight cotton fabric by an artist-designer who
bases her textile work on her limited-edition linocut
and wood engraving prints. Skeletal plant forms
seen against the sea and sky of north Norfolk and
the Scottish Highlands provide continual inspiration.

Phyllis Barron and Dorothy Larcher
Large Palm, 1920s–30s
Hand block-printed onto organdie, this design was intended for dress fabric or maybe for light summer curtains. Making wooden handmade blocks is a time-consuming and highly skilled process, and these two artisans became adept at it, making and printing hundreds of yards of fabric for personal and commercial use.

Phyllis Barron and Dorothy Larcher
1930s–40s
An unnamed lozenge pattern and a block of eight
stars, together with a stencil design, have all been
hand block-printed in black iron liquor onto undyed
cotton organdie.

Peter Osborne and Antony Little
Trifid, 1970
A wallpaper hand screen-printed onto silver metallic paper from the *Painted Lady* range by the firm of Osborne & Little, which was started by these two brothers-in-law with 'a shared passion for creativity and instinct for business', in London's Chelsea district in 1968.

Rob Ryan
We Don't Fly North, 2008
An extraordinarily intricate work by this artist who painstakingly hand cuts delicate papers. The artist comments: 'This is quite a large papercut that took forever to do. All those stars and birds!'

Susan Williams-Ellis for Portmeirion Pottery
Magic City, 1966
A fabulous design of dark, mysterious and exotic roof and window shapes, inspired by the artist's travels, has been used to decorate this 'serif'-shape ceramic coffee set. It was probably the most popular design of its time and is now extremely sought-after by collectors. Susan was the daughter of Sir Clough Williams-Ellis who created the fantastic Portmeirion village in North Wales.

Anonymous
1930s
A fine, black line design for a gentleman's roller-printed silk scarf, with an interlocked border and filling patterns, which draw on elements inspired by Gothic designs.

Jessie Tait for Midwinter Pottery
Zambesi, 1956
Designed by the gifted painter and designer
Jessie Tait, this hand-painted design of African-
inspired wavy lines with bright red detailing was an
instant success when it was launched, and it was
subsequently widely imitated by competitors.

Anonymous for Alfred Meakin
Swirl, 1950s
An interesting curling graphic pattern, transfer-printed onto earthenware china for the firm of Alfred Meakin, who continued to produce ceramics aimed specifically at the North American market throughout the 1950s.

Anonymous
1950s
Loosely rendered flowers in modulated shades
of grey, with a few highlighted areas of blue and
magenta, are screen-printed onto a silk satin
fashion fabric.

Rob Ryan
Boat couple, 2007
A limited-edition screen print derived from one
of his remarkable intricate papercuts, this artist's
designs have appeared on a number of substrates,
from ceramics to sneakers. In addition he has
designed book jackets, laser-cut embroidery for
wedding dresses, T-shirts and more!

Zandra Rhodes
Stalactite, 1966
A seminal printed cotton fabric design by Zandra
Rhodes for Heal Fabrics Ltd. Considered too
outrageous by the traditional British textile
manufacturers, Zandra's own lifestyle has proved to
be as dramatic, glamorous and extroverted as her
designs. With her brightly coloured hair, theatrical
make-up and art jewellery, she has stamped her
identity on the international world of fashion.

Peter Osborne and Antony Little
Strawberry Hill, 1970
Clearly derived from the Gothic and medieval style of decoration, this hand-printed wallpaper is by Osborne & Little. The pattern title is doubtless inspired by 'Strawberry Hill', the fancifully Gothic villa built by Horace Walpole in London in the 18th century, which has lent its name to ornate variations of Gothic style architecture.

Anonymous (American School)
1940s
Superbly designed in stark black and white, this
screen-printed design has been very cleverly
constructed, so that each section of the design
is interconnected with every other part, while
maintaining the fine balance between the areas
of pattern.

Wedgwood & Co. of Tunstall
Barbeque, 1957
Enoch Wedgwood, a distant relative of the famous
Josiah Wedgwood, formed this company in 1860
and continued to produce high-quality ceramics
for the home and export market until their
amalgamation with the Wedgwood Group in 1980.

Phyllis Barron and Dorothy Larcher
1920s–30s
Two unnamed blocks have been hand block-printed
onto undyed organdie cotton. At the time, designs
like this would have been considered most suitable
for cushions and tablecloths.

Linda Sjunnesson for Spira
Trädgård, 2007
Mountains, rocks and a snowy landscape are the motifs used on a melamine-coated tray, which has been designed by an imaginative Scandinavian design team.

Josef Hoffmann
1910–15
Josef Hoffmann was a co-founder and artistic
director of the Wiener Werkstätte from 1903–31.
His design style was one of skilfully understated
minimalism and often comprised angular and
geometric motifs, as in this example.

Anonymous
c.1980s
Tessellating designs of this kind are found all over
Southeast Asia. This contemporary fabric, hand
block-printed in indigo, has the ancient swastika,
or good-luck symbol, in its centre.

Eduardo Paolozzi and Nigel Henderson for Hammer Prints
c.1954
A graphic and surreal textile design, this screen-printed fabric was produced around the time of *Painting into Textiles*, an influential exhibition held at the Institute of Contemporary Arts, London, in 1953, which promoted British artists and their involvement in textile design.

Linda Sjunnesson for Spira
Katja, 2007
Bulbous organic shapes are perched on branches
in an asymmetrical textile design for children's
furnishings. When printed as both sides of a mirror
image, the pattern also makes handsome wallpaper.

Åsa Erickson for Spira
Skärva, 2008
A geometric pattern of intersecting lines makes a dazzling design for wallpapers and fabrics. The pattern also appears on a range of melamine-coated kitchen accessories.

Rachel Goodchild
White Scottie Dogs, 2006
Inspired by vintage fashion fabrics, these delightful 'Scottie' dogs were created by cutting their shapes out of handmade mulberry paper. The artist then attached ribbon for each collar to give them a raised texture.

Florence Broadhurst
1960s–70s
Peacock feathers, with their distinctive silhouette
and vibrant colouring, provide excellent possibilities
for surface pattern designs or objets d'art and were
particularly favoured by the Aesthetic Movement
of the early 1900s. In this instance, they appear as
motifs on a monochromatic design for wallpaper.

Anonymous for Langley Printworks
1951–52
A floral design given extra gravitas by being hand screen-printed in black on white, this is a quarter design for a ladies headscarf.

Eley Kishimoto
Flash, 1995
This is the black version of London design duo
Eley Kishimoto's signature design, which they have
applied to every possible surface imaginable, from
cars to toys to sneakers. 'This print is like a stamp of
approval, or a virus, that travels onto things that we
like!' says Mark Eley.

Reiko Sudo for Nuno Corporation
Bounteous Rain, 2006
A working drawing by this visionary Japanese
designer whose textiles have been said to
have 'visual wit, technical understanding and
wild fearlessness'. Her combination of complex
technologies, traditional techniques and new
finishing processes has created extraordinary visual
effects for textiles within interiors, fashion and art.

Arnold Lever
1951
Featuring a pattern based on the crystal structure diagram of haemoglobin, this is a screen-printed silk fabric. The designs were chosen for the important Festival of Britain exhibition because, as Mark Hartland Thomas said at the time: 'They are derived from nature – although it is nature at a submicroscopic scale not previously revealed.'

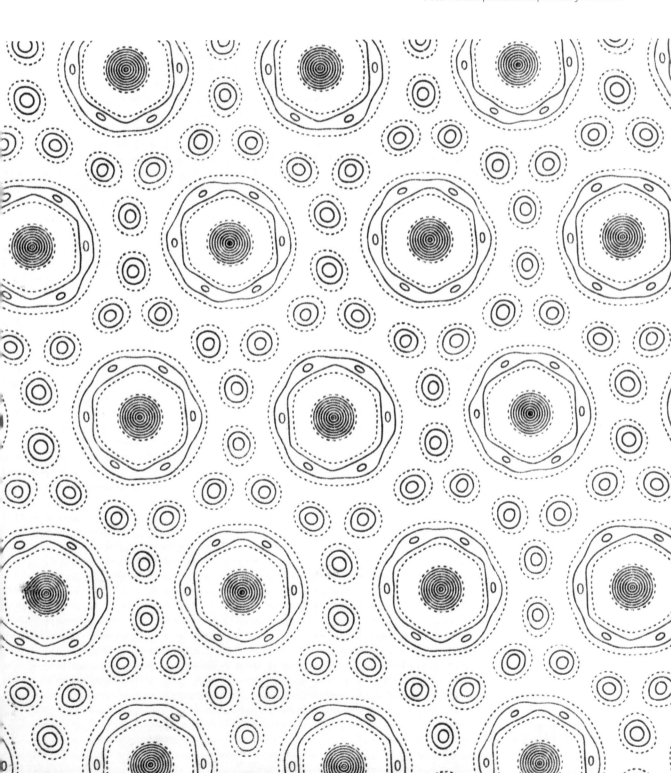

Contacts

Meg Andrews
meg@meg-andrews.com
www.meg-andrews.com

Laura Ashley
info@lauraashley.com
www.lauraashley.com

Kim Barnett
birds.in.skirts@googlemail.com

Linda Brassington
l.brassington@ucreative.ac.uk
www.ucreative.ac.uk

Florence Broadhurst
sales@signatureprints.com.au
www.signatureprints.com.au

Pippa Caley
pippa@pippacaley.com
www.pippacaley.com

Francesca Chiorando
francescachiorando@hotmail.com
http://fchiorando.blogspot.com

Drusilla Cole
druvcole@aol.com
www.drusillacole.co.uk

Cole and Son
(Wallpapers) Ltd
customer.service@cole-
and-son.com
www.cole-and-son.com

Sarah Colson
sscolson@gmail.com
www.interdisciplinary
textiledesign.com

Crafts Study Centre,
University for the Creative
Arts at Farnham
craftscentre@ucreative.ac.uk
www.csc.ucreative.ac.uk

Samantha Doe
samanthadoe142@hotmail.com
www.rugmark.org.uk/news/
sam_doe_profile.pdf

Ella Doran
info@elladoran.co.uk
www.elladoran.co.uk

Mark Eley
info@eleykishimoto.com
www.eleykishimoto.com

Maija Fagerlund
maija.fagerlund@elisanet.fi
www.maijafagerlund.com

Kaffe Fassett
info@kaffefassett.com
www.kaffefassett.com

Hannah Firmin
hannah@hmfirmin.eclipse.co.uk
www.illustrationweb.com/
HannahFirmin

Marie-Noëlle Fontan
manoellefontan@hotmail.com
www.marie-noelle-fontan.com

Josef Frank
info@svenskttenn.se
www.svenskttenn.se

Chloe Geary
clogeary@aol.com
www.clogeary.blogspot.com

Alexander Girard
info@maximodesign.com
www.maximodesign.com

Rachel Goodchild
info@rachelgoodchild.com
www.rachelgoodchild.com

Tricia Guild
info@designersguild.com
www.designersguild.com

Hennie Haworth
henniehaworth@hotmail.com
www.henniehaworth.co.uk

Mark Hearld
info@stjudes.co.uk
www.stjudes.co.uk

Tobie Jennings
tobie-jennings@hotmail.co.uk
t.jennings@me.com

Seiko Kinoshita
seikokino@yahoo.com
www.seikokinoshita.com

Wakako Kishimoto
info@eleykishimoto.com
www.eleykishimoto.com

Angie Lewin
info@stjudes.co.uk
www.stjudes.co.uk

Antony Little
oandl@osborneandlittle.com
www.osborneandlittle.com

Macclesfield Silk Museum
info@macclesfield.silk.museum
www.macclesfield.silk.museum

Marimekko
info@marimekko.fi
www.marimekko.com

máXimo: Art and
Design Research
info@maximodesign.com
www.maximodesign.com

The Henry Moore Foundation
info@henry-moore-fdn.co.uk
www.henry-moore-fdn.co.uk

Nuno Corporation
info@nuno.com
www.nuno.com/home.html

Peter Osborne
oandl@osborneandlittle.com
www.osborneandlittle.com

James Pegg
jamesdpegg@googlemail.com

Minä Perhonen
info@mina-perhonen.jp
www.mina-perhonen.jp

The Potteries Museum
and Art Gallery
museums@stoke.gov.uk
www.stokemuseums.org.
uk/pmag

Zandra Rhodes
zrhodesent@aol.com
www.zandrarhodes.com

Rob Ryan
ryanton17@hotmail.com
www.misterrob.co.uk

Signature Prints
sales@signatureprints.com.au
www.signatureprints.com.au

Spira
anna.tareby@spirainredning.se
www.spirainredning.se

St Jude's
info@stjudes.co.uk
www.stjudes.co.uk

Reiko Sudo
info@nuno.com
www.nuno.com/home.html

Svenskt Tenn
info@svenskttenn.se
www.svenskttenn.se

Rita Trefois
rita.trefois@pandora.be
http://users.telenet.be/
ritatrefois-batikart.be

University of the Arts London,
CSM & Study Collection
info@csm.arts.ac.uk
www.csm.arts.ac.uk

V & A Museum
textilesandfashion@vam.ac.uk
www.vam.ac.uk

Walcot Hall
enquiries@walcothall.co.uk
www.walcothall.co.uk

Worcester Porcelain Museum
info@worcesterporcelain
museum.org.uk
www.worcesterporcelain
museum.org.uk

Bibliography

Ames, Frank, *The Kashmir Shawl*, Suffolk: Antique Collectors' Club, 1986

Cole, Drusilla, *1000 Patterns*, London: A&C Black, 2003

Cole, Drusilla, *Textiles Now*, London: Laurence King, 2008

Collins, Louanne, *Macclesfield Silk Museums: A Look at the Collections*: Macclesfield Museum Trust, 2000

Collins, Louanne and Stevenson, Moira, *Silk: Sarsenets, Satins, Steels & Stripes*: Macclesfield Museum Trust, 2000

Dupont-Auberville, M., *Classic Textile Designs*, London: Studio Editions, 1996

Feldman, Anita (ed.), *Henry Moore Textiles*, Aldershot: Lund Humphries, 2008

Fogg, Marnie, *Print in Fashion*, London: Batsford, 2006

Hardy, Alain-René, *Art Deco Textiles*, London: Thames & Hudson, 2003

Horn, Richard, *Fifties Style*, Kent: Columbus Books, 1985

Jackson, Lesley, *From Atoms to Patterns*, London: Richard Dennis Publications in association with Wellcome Collection, 2008

Jenkins, Steven, *Midwinter Pottery*, Somerset: Richard Dennis, 2003

Kerry, Sue, *Twentieth Century Textiles Part II*, Suffolk, UK: Francesca Galloway in association with the Antique Collectors' Club, 2007

Meller, Susan and Elffers, Joost, *Textile Designs*, London: Thames & Hudson, 1991

Nakano, Eisha and Stephan, Barbara B., *Japanese Stencil Dyeing*, Tokyo: Weatherhill, 1982

Poli, Doretta Davanzo, *Twentieth-century Fabrics*, Milan: Skira Editore, 2007

Raynor, Geoffrey et al, *Artists' Textiles in Britain 1945–70*, London: Antique Collectors' Club, 2003

Schoeser, Mary and Rufey, Celia, *English and American Textiles*, New York: Thames & Hudson, 1989

Sykas, Philip Anthony, *The Secret Life of Textiles*, Manchester: Bolton Museums, 2005

Yasinskaya I., *Soviet Textile Design*, London: Thames & Hudson, 1983

Picture Credits

The author and publisher would like to thank the following individuals, institutions and picture libraries for providing photographic images for use in this book. Every effort has been made to trace the copyright holders. We apologise in advance for any unintentional omissions and would be pleased to insert the appropriate acknowledgements in any subsequent edition of this publication.

Pp 2–3 Minä Perhonen, Japan; p4 Hennie Haworth; p6 Worcester Porcelain Museum; p9 Rita Trefois; p10 © The Design Library, New York, USA/Bridgeman Art Library London; p11 Rob Ryan; p13 © The Design Library, New York, USA/Bridgeman Art Library London; p15L Design Council Slide Collection at Manchester Metropolitan University, © Design Council; p15R © Dan Bosence/Crafts Study Centre, University for the Creative Arts, Farnham/2008. www.vads.ac.uk; p16 St Jude's; p17L © Ella Doran 2008; p17R Crafts Study Centre, University for the Creative Arts, Farnham/2008; p18L The Textiles Collection, University for the Creative Arts at Farnham/© Linda Brassington; p18R The Textiles Collection, University for the Creative Arts at Farnham.; p19 The Whitworth Art Gallery, The University of Manchester; p20L Crafts Study Centre, University for the Creative Arts, Farnham/2008.; p20R © V&A Images, Victoria & Albert Museum; p21 Crafts Study Centre, University for the Creative Arts, Farnham/2008.; p22 Victoria & Albert Museum, London, UK/Bridgeman Art Library London; p25 Treble Clef, Zigzag and Oval Safety Pins 1946–47. Reproduced by permission of the Henry Moore Foundation. TEX 12.8, rayon, printed by ASCHER, photo: Matt Pia; p30 © Warner Textile Archive, Braintree District Museum & Study Trust Ltd; pp31–32 Crafts Study Centre, University for the Creative Arts, Farnham/2008.; p33 © Alexander Girard ®. Photo provided by máXimo: Art and Design Research; p34 Worcester Porcelain Museum; p36L Copyright CDMT (Quico Ortega); p36R Marie-Noëlle Fontan. Photo: Guillermo Escalon; p37 Winter: Hannah Firmin/Illustrationweb. (Images part of a series for the Nightingale Project which organises exhibitions at the South Kensington & Chelsea Mental Health Centre); p39L Design Council Slide Collection at Manchester Metropolitan University/©V&A Images, Victoria & Albert Museum; p39R Copyright CDMT (Quico Ortega); p43 James D. Pegg; p44 © V&A Images, Victoria & Albert Museum; p46 John Bethell/ The Bridgeman Art Library; p47 The Textiles Collection, University for the Creative Arts at Farnham.; pp48–49 Francesca Chiorando; p50 The Art Archive/Private Collection/Gianni Dagli Orti; p52 © Tokyo Fuji Art Museum, Tokyo, Japan /The Bridgeman Art Library; p54L © V&A Images, Victoria & Albert Museum; p54R Museum of Domestic Design & Architecture, Middlesex University; p55 Seiko Kinoshita. Photo: Paula Kirby; p57 © Spira. www.spirainredning.se; p58 Crafts Study Centre, University for the Creative Arts, Farnham/2008.; p59L akg-images; pp60–61 Chloe Geary; p62 © Rachel Goodchild, Designer. www.rachelgoodchild.

LAURENCE KING

Published in 2009 by
Laurence King Publishing Ltd
361–373 City Road
London EC1V 1LR
Tel +44 20 7841 6900
Fax +44 20 7841 6910
E-mail: enquiries@laurenceking.com
www.laurenceking.com

A catalogue record for this book is available from
the British Library.

ISBN 978 1 85669 621 0

Designed by Rudd Studio
Picture Research by Kate Lockley

Printed in Singapore

Dedication

This is especially dedicated to my gorgeous
grandson, Jack Merlin Carey, with love and
best wishes.

Acknowledgements

I would like to give sincere thanks to all the
designers, artists, craftsmen and craftswomen,
past and present, who, through their artistry and
dedication, have made this book possible.

In addition, I would like to give thanks to the team
at Laurence King Publishing, in particular Helen
Evans and Zoe Antoniou, for their support and
guidance, and to Eleanor Ridsdale of Rudd Studio for
her excellent design skills. In addition, appreciative
thanks must go to my tireless researcher Kate
Lockley, who has worked so hard on this project.

A number of the patterns originate from historic
manufacturers' pattern books, now held in
museum archives. These precious records have
been invaluable in compiling this book and proved
to be a source of patterns of astonishing richness
and diversity. I would like to give special thanks to
Anabel Wills, archivist of Macclesfield Silk Museum
for her patience and assistance, and to Richard de
Peyer, Director of the Silk Museum. Grateful thanks
also to Wendy Cook, curator of the Worcester
Porcelain Museum, for her help and efficiency,
and to the Woodbine Parish family of Walcot Hall,
Shropshire, for generously giving me access to their
vintage fabric collection.

I would also like to thank my friends Rosie Byrd,
Sue Davies and Jennifer Hepke for sharing their
textiles with me.

Lastly, I would like to thank my lovely daughters
Emily and Peggy for their continued support
and love.